The
DELIBERATE
and
COURAGEOUS
PRINCIPAL

Ten Leadership
Actions and Skills
to Create
High-Achieving
Schools

RHONDA J. ROOS

FOREWORD BY TODD WHITAKER

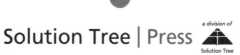

Solution Tree | Press

555 North Morton Street
Bloomington, IN 47404
800.733.6786 (toll free) / 812.336.7700
FAX: 812.336.7790

email: info@SolutionTree.com
SolutionTree.com

Visit **go.SolutionTree.com/leadership** to download the free reproducibles in this book.

Printed in the United States of America

Library of Congress Cataloging-in-Publication Data

Names: Roos, Rhonda J., author.
Title: The deliberate and courageous principal : ten leadership actions and
   skills to create high-achieving schools / Rhonda J. Roos.
Description: Bloomington, IN : Solution Tree Press, [2022] | Includes
   bibliographical references and index.
Identifiers: LCCN 2021037148 (print) | LCCN 2021037149 (ebook) | ISBN
   9781952812354 (paperback) | ISBN 9781952812361 (ebook)
Subjects: LCSH: School principals. | Educational leadership. |
   Teacher-principal relationships.
Classification: LCC LB2831.9 .R66 2022 (print) | LCC LB2831.9 (ebook) |
   DDC 371.2/011--dc23
LC record available at https://lccn.loc.gov/2021037148
LC ebook record available at https://lccn.loc.gov/2021037149

Solution Tree
Jeffrey C. Jones, CEO
Edmund M. Ackerman, President

Solution Tree Press
President and Publisher: Douglas M. Rife
Associate Publisher: Sarah Payne-Mills
Art Director: Rian Anderson
Managing Production Editor: Kendra Slayton
Editorial Director: Todd Brakke
Copy Chief: Jessi Finn
Production Editor: Miranda Addonizio
Content Development Specialist: Amy Rubenstein
Acquisitions Editor: Sarah Jubar
Copy Editor: Jessi Finn
Proofreader: Evie Madsen
Text and Cover Designer: Laura Cox
Editorial Assistants: Sarah Ludwig and Elijah Oates

This book is dedicated to my two-year-old granddaughter,
Eliza Kallie, who has taught me so much already.
All along your journey, Eliza, may you have the
deliberate and courageous principals you so deserve.

Acknowledgments

My husband Vic for always taking such good care of my heart.

My daughter Megan and son Keigan for bringing nothing but joy to my life and inspiring me to be a better human being.

These special people who graciously took their time to read this manuscript in the very early stages. I'm forever grateful to each of them.

- My dear friends, Diane, Janet, John, and Linda for all of their critical feedback

- My daughter Megan for being my very first reviewer (that was painful)

- My sister Becky (a principal too) for her detailed suggestions

- My daughter-in-law Katy for helping me think through the initial stages of the visual design

- My son-in-law Josh for listening to all the research stories

- My ninety-year-old dad who told me to make the ending better (I did)

- My content editor Amy for examining my thinking and becoming a friend in the process

And my amazing family—my children and their spouses (Meg and Josh, Keigan and Katy), my precious granddaughters, my parents, three sisters, nieces and nephews, in-laws, and three bonus kids Carson, Presley, and Camden! I'm so grateful for our whole, big, fabulous, never-could-have-dreamt-it family.

Solution Tree Press would like to thank the following reviewers:

Abbey Campbell
Principal
Silver Creek Primary School
Sellersburg, Indiana

Molly Capps
Principal
McDeeds Creek Elementary
Southern Pines, North Carolina

Craig Mah
District Principal of School Services and
Special Projects
Coquitlam School District
Coquitlam, British Columbia, Canada

Blane McCann
Educational Consultant
Omaha, Nebraska

Brad Neuendorf
Principal
Lander Valley High School
Lander, Wyoming

David Robertson
Assistant Superintendent
Warsaw Community Schools
Warsaw, Indiana

Kim Timmerman
Principal
Adel Desoto Minburn Middle School
Adel, Iowa

Edward Velez
Principal
John F. Kennedy High School
Fremont, California

Visit **go.SolutionTree.com/leadership** to
download the free reproducibles in this book.

Table of Contents

Reproducibles are in italics.

About the Author

 **Rhonda J. Roos, PhD,** is an educational consultant who coaches principals, district leaders, and administrative teams in the complex and ever-challenging work of leading schools. She is a former director of middle schools in New Albany, Indiana, where she led curricular improvement, aligning those efforts with the district's progress in becoming a professional learning community. Rhonda has been an educator since 1983, serving as a guidance counselor, English teacher, middle school principal, and district administrator. She has taught graduate courses on leadership at Indiana University Southeast in New Albany, Indiana, and Spalding University in Louisville, Kentucky. Rhonda also works with organizations outside the education realm to assist them in creating healthy teams, no matter the organizations' mission.

Rhonda serves on the leadership team of the Indiana Principal Leadership Institute and is a regular keynote speaker. Her honors include the 2009 Indiana Middle School Principal of the Year, the 2011 Solution Tree Redefining Excellence District Award, and the 2015 Indiana University Southeast Educator of the Year. Rhonda completed her dissertation, "An Examination of Principals in Effective High-Poverty Middle Schools With High Achievement," in 2014, and she coauthored an article in the National Association of Secondary School Principals' *NASSP Bulletin* titled "Brain Compatible Secondary Schools: The Visionary Principal's Role."

Rhonda received a bachelor's degree in English from Eastern Kentucky University, a master's degree in counseling from Western Kentucky University, her administrative license through the Experiential Program for Preparing School Principals (EPPSP) at Butler University, and her education specialist degree and doctorate from Indiana State University. Rhonda is also a Myers-Briggs Type Indicator (MBTI) certified trainer.

Rhonda lives in Louisville, Kentucky, with her husband, Vic.

To book Rhonda J. Roos for professional development, contact pd@SolutionTree.com.

Foreword

By Todd Whitaker

The goal of this book is to inspire educational leaders to become better. A clear vision and focus, based on what is ultimately best for our students, is a central theme. I met Rhonda when I had the good fortune to serve as her dissertation chair and had the honor of working with her for two years. She's personable, genuine, and believes that students will have trouble achieving at high levels unless educators exhibit specific actions and skills. Rhonda clarifies the work that really matters. That's what you'll come to understand in this book: the work of ten specific actions and skills. Rhonda shares her own experiences as well as some of the research around these topics as she tries to help readers strengthen their understanding of the concepts. I enjoyed reading her personal stories, the step-by-step practical tools, and the ready-to-use reproducibles that are included. It can be challenging work, but Rhonda clearly describes the impact it can have on everyone involved.

Part 1 of this book starts with five deliberate actions all principals must embrace to drive improvements in their schools. Each one of these actions builds on the next. After you read each chapter, you can work through the reproducibles, and then you'll be able to spend some time reflecting on how you could strengthen each action in your own leadership journey.

Part 2 of this book is about the five courageous skills every principal must demonstrate. These skills are meant to be embedded into all the work in part 1 that explains the deliberate actions. You'll sense Rhonda's firm belief that these skills are equally as important as the actions. It is quite difficult to be an effective leader without both facets.

I recommend the book for all principals—new and experienced alike. It is also relevant for district leaders to help guide their principals and establish a high degree of consistency among each of the schools in their district. And in addition to all that, it's a valuable resource for teachers who are informally and formally leading within their schools.

This book is based on the framework of Rhonda's educational professional development work. Her experience, frustrations, triumphs, and key learnings throughout her career as a teacher, principal, and district administrator have been captured wonderfully in this book. *The Deliberate and Courageous Principal* is a valuable resource for leading a school. Rhonda's leadership style is real, and this resource enables readers to replicate her approach. You'll learn from her and with her. This book will help school leaders improve. Your team will grow, and your students will reap the benefits.

Introduction

Exhaustion had taken over. I was a school principal, and I was so tired. Not tired from the expected things, like overseeing a building of a thousand students, making sure schedules were ready, organizing teacher meetings, responding to parent concerns, or cheering for students at way too many ball games. No, those things weren't the ultimate cause of my exhaustion.

I was tired from asking myself that ever-present question running through my mind: "Am I doing what I'm supposed to be doing?"

That question hung over my being like my winter coat on early morning bus duty. For several years, I questioned myself almost every day. That incessant question was usually joined by others.

- "Am I doing the things that principals of high-achieving schools do?"
- "What is the secret to leading a successful school, where students achieve at high levels and staff members work together to do whatever it takes for the school to thrive?"
- "Exactly what makes some principals able to achieve such success?"

This book answers those questions for principals at all levels: elementary, middle, and high school. Based on research from others, along with research and experience of my own, this book will provide clear direction for new principals, aspiring principals, principals facing challenges, and other education leaders. We'll look at five essential leadership *actions* and five essential leadership *skills* that principals must have in place if they want to lead schools where students achieve at high levels.

You may ask, "Why actions *and* skills? What's the difference?" In order for their schools to be successful, principals must be capable of leading them in two distinct ways, which are made possible by the essential leadership actions and skills. First, principals need the essential *actions* to answer the question, "Do I know what I'm doing?" And second, they need the essential *skills* to answer the question, "Can I lead people to accomplish what I'm doing?"

In order for an organization to succeed, it must achieve two criteria: the organization must be (1) smart and (2) healthy. Being smart means having the technical competence to deal with the critical aspects of the organization. However, Patrick Lencioni (2012), founder and president of the Table Group, a firm dedicated to helping leaders improve their organizational health, writes that "being smart is only half the equation. Yet somehow it occupies almost all the time, energy, and attention of most executives. The other half of the equation, the one that is largely neglected, is about being healthy" (p. 5). In healthy school districts and schools, leaders have largely eliminated the politics and confusion. People know what to do, understand clearly their role in the school, have strong morale, and trust in their leaders. The work moves forward. In this kind of healthy work environment, no one wants to leave. But sometimes organizational health is neglected because leaders think it sounds easy. It may seem simple, but that doesn't mean it's easy to do. Building a healthy organization takes discipline. It's uncomfortable to walk into tense circumstances and address conflict. It's hard to hold people accountable. It's tough to consistently maintain a positive outlook. It's not easy, and it takes courage. The root of the word *courage* is *cor*: the Latin word for "heart" (Courage, n.d.). In one of its earliest forms, the word *courage* meant to speak one's mind by telling all the heart (Brown, 2007). Maybe poet Maya Angelou said it best when she said, "Courage is the most important of all the virtues. Because without courage, you can't practice any other virtue consistently" (as cited in Diaz, 2017). When leaders are willing to be courageous enough to devote their energy to the health of their organizations, the results are undeniable.

Part 1 of this book addresses the smart actions that school leaders must take with deliberateness, and part 2 takes on the healthy skills that school leaders must embed with all the courage they can muster. Read on for a breakdown of each of these actions and skills, and turn to page 8 for a one-page graphic organizer on which you can take notes right in the book or that you can copy or download to keep with you as you read to record your thoughts.

Part 1: Essential Leadership Actions

Part 1 comprises five chapters that focus on the five essential *actions* of principals. These deliberate actions focus on the safe and predictable work that we've been trained to do as educators and that we feel most comfortable doing. They involve curricular initiatives, school discipline programs, finances, effective meetings, and development of each system within the school. At the end of each chapter, you will find reproducibles to help you reflect on and think through learnings from the chapter. The actions of each chapter build upon one another. Think of the chapters as a process for getting the essential pieces in place for your school.

Chapter 1: Establish a Vision Focused on Learning

In order for schools to function at their highest level, they need a vision to help guide them from their current level of achievement to future possibilities of growth. A vision can challenge everyone in the organization to think and operate differently. As a leader, you can drive this growth. You can rally your staff to see a better future. You can demonstrate your passion for progress and dissatisfaction for the status quo. This chapter offers five foundational questions to help you tackle the often underused action of establishing a school vision. These questions include (1) What is a vision?; (2) Why have a vision?; (3) What do you need to know before you create the vision?; (4) How do you create your school's vision?; and (5) When do you utilize the vision? The answers to these five questions can help you through a step-by-step process to better prepare to establish your school's vision and begin your school's journey of continued growth.

Chapter 2: Clarify the Essential Work

Once you have established a vision, the next step is to clarify the essential work that will help keep your focus on student learning. Begin by creating a comprehensive inventory of all the work that needs to be done for your school to be successful. Next, lead your staff in prioritizing the critical work for the semester and providing clarity so all staff members know exactly what work needs to be accomplished and what individual role they have in that work. It is critical that leaders take this action of clarifying the work for the organization. Chapter 2 offers suggestions as you set out to do the work of this all-too-commonly missing component of principal leadership.

Chapter 3: Create Teams to Move the Work Forward

Now that you have set the school's vision and clarified the essential work, it's time to create teams to assist your school in accomplishing this work. This chapter establishes the key foundations of a team by clearly defining what a team is and how team members work together, and it introduces three key understandings that you, as school leader, must have of your school's leadership team: you must (1) have clarity on the leadership team's purpose and members' responsibilities; (2) select the right members for your leadership team; and (3) get the right number of people on your leadership team. The chapter closes with a look at the significance of your teacher leaders and four crucial actions in building that team: (1) select wisely, (2) provide training, (3) check in regularly, and (4) create a professional development calendar.

Chapter 4: Take Action Instead of Being Busy

To help you succeed, time management skills are critical. Principals must painstakingly review how they spend the minutes of their days. This chapter will help you come to understand the difference between being busy and taking action. There are three focus areas that you should consider in your time management: (1) building the systems of your systems list, (2) managing time efficiently, and (3) creating your principal monthly guide. Positive changes and outcomes can come only when you are aware of the minutes in each school day and then use those minutes to create the most high-quality and rigorous learning environment.

Chapter 5: Lead Effective Meetings

The first four chapters establish how effective principals work to establish a vision, clarify the essential work, create teams, and take action. The fifth essential leadership action is to lead effective meetings that ground the work of your school. Meetings have come to have a negative connotation in most school settings. Poorly run meetings can be frustrating and take up entirely too much time. You

[Handwritten margin notes: "VISION", "Create a comprehensive inventory of what you need to do for your school to be successful.", "ESSENTIAL WORK", "Clarity when communicating directives to staff. All staff know exactly what work needs to be done and their role", "Time Management skills are imperative to succeed.", "Take Action instead of Being Busy", "Poorly run meetings can be frustrating and take up too much time."]

must know how to organize your meetings and create meaning for each of them so that they have a fundamental impact on the work of your school. Well-run meetings accomplish critical work. This chapter discusses six foundational meetings: (1) daily check-in meeting, (2) weekly office team meeting, (3) topical meeting, (4) biweekly leadership team meeting, (5) monthly faculty meeting, and (6) semester off-site meeting.

Part 2: Essential Leadership Skills

Part 2 comprises five chapters focusing on five essential *skills* of principals. These are the healthy, empowering skills of leadership—they require courage. Many principals struggle when it comes to using and honing these particular skills. The work of embedding these emotional, compassionate leadership skills is messier than the concrete leadership actions of part 1. It moves from answering the question, "Do I know what I'm doing?" to answering the question, "Can I lead people to accomplish what I'm doing?" Many leaders refer to these skills as *soft skills*, but let's be clear. These skills are extremely complex and difficult to hone, and they are just as essential as the principal actions. They are anything but soft.

Daniel Goleman (2019), psychologist and codeveloper of the Goleman Emotional Intelligence coaching program, suggests that effective leaders are alike in one critical way—they have emotional intelligence:

> It's not that IQ and technical skills are irrelevant. They do matter, but mainly as "threshold capabilities"; that is, they are the entry-level requirements for executive positions. But my research, along with other recent studies, clearly shows that emotional intelligence is the sine qua non of leadership. Without it, a person can have the best training in the world, an incisive, analytical mind, and an endless supply of smart ideas, but [that person] still won't make a great leader. (pp. 4–5)

The five leadership skills require emotional intelligence from school leaders. Effective principals must fully understand that the five essential leadership actions of part 1 are entry-level components of being a principal. Part 2 shifts to a deeper level and discusses the fundamentals of embedding the five essential leadership skills into your daily practice. Again, you can view the leadership actions in part 1 as a process, building from one chapter to the next. The leadership skills of part 2 are a little different; they must be embedded, day in and day out, in your daily work. They're certainly not a simple addition to consider at the end of the day. I recommend taking the necessary time to read all about the five skills before beginning the leadership actions in the first five chapters. Leaders in healthy organizations wouldn't think of taking action without these skills. Strengthen each one. Weave each of them into your work. Give them their necessary and deserved place, right alongside the actions. Allow them to deepen and sustain your leadership each step of the way.

Chapter 6: Build Relationships

In order to accomplish the leadership actions presented in part 1, the skill of building relationships is essential. Schools are people-driven organizations, and principals must

prioritize the work of building relationships with staff members. This chapter will look at the work of principals in building trust and having difficult conversations. At the end of the day, when staff members trust their principal, difficult conversations can occur, building and strengthening the relationships even further. The chapter closes with knowing your people. This is the simple but often-neglected act of taking time to check in on staff members, ask about their families, and make sure all understand the significant contribution they make to the school.

[handwritten margin note: Check in with staff, ask about their families, and ensure they understand the significant contribution they make to the school.]

Chapter 7: Reframe Conflict

Conflict can have such a negative connotation. This chapter will encourage you to entirely reframe your way of thinking about conflict. Being an effective principal means coming to the realization that conflict will always be part of your leadership. Learning to address all kinds of conflict and to even dig for conflict at times are both essential pieces of reframing it. You can learn to not only address the conflict in your school but also adjust your perspective so you see the opportunities that can arise from that conflict. How do you address conflict? How do you make the tough decisions that are sometimes required with conflict? Chapter 7 offers suggestions for tackling these questions and others.

[handwritten margin note: Address conflict and even dig for conflict at times]

Chapter 8: Hold People Accountable

Accountability in leadership is missing in many schools, and principals often share with me that it is the most difficult skill to master. Accountability begins with clear expectations. Staff members deserve these clear expectations, and they deserve leaders who will hold the staff accountable while also holding themselves accountable. Schools need leaders to be strong in this area of accountability because it makes a real difference. Why? Because accountable principals take responsibility for their actions and behaviors. And they also hold others accountable so their school can grow, flourish, and become incredibly healthy.

[handwritten margin note: Be accountable for my actions and behaviors, hold others accountable with clear expectations]

Chapter 9: Lean Into the Positive

Let's face it. Stress comes with the role of being a school leader. Standing strong in your leadership to clearly face all the challenges and negative aspects of leading a school can be exhausting. This chapter will provide tools to help you lean into the positive amid your challenging work. Six tools are available to help you lead without exacerbating the stresses inherent in your role. Read about each tool, and hopefully dig further into the research behind the ones that resonate with you.

Chapter 10: Turn Inward

This intentionally short chapter is for you to collect your thoughts and begin thinking about the way you take care of yourself. Consider it a wrapping-up respite! So many principals get caught in the never-ending cycle of caring for others: staff, students, parents, and community members, not to mention their own families. This chapter includes three strategies for your consideration to build healthy habits in your leadership: (1) getting quiet each day, (2) journaling, and (3) connecting with a colleague. This final chapter's focus is simple: you can't take care of your staff and school unless you're taking care of yourself.

The Power of Principals

As we begin to explore the essential actions and skills of principals in high-achieving schools, one basic understanding must be clear: principals make a huge difference throughout their schools, including an influence on student test scores (when reviewing gains throughout their tenure) and so much more! In a research report commissioned by the Wallace Foundation, the authors write:

> Effective principals are at least as important for student achievement as previous reports have included—and in fact, their importance may not have been stated strongly enough. . . . We now have rigorous, arguably causal studies based on longitudinal data that can estimate the size of principal's effect on achievement. Effective principals have large effects. Replacing a below-average principal (at the 25th percentile) with an above-average one (at the 75th percentile) would increase the typical student's learning by nearly three months in both math and reading annually. (Grissom, Egalite, & Lindsay, 2021, p. 91)

In addition, Kristian Holden (2018), researcher with the American Institutes for Research, writes that "research suggests positive associations between principals' time use [and] organizational management skills . . . [and] principal quality also appears to play an important role in teacher turnover and differential retention of effective teachers" (p. i). It's clear that the actions and skills of principals lead to school achievement in multiple ways.

A fundamental path to achievement is the way leaders work with teachers to build collective success. High-achieving principals are keenly aware that the impact of their work is what creates this collaborative environment for teachers. These principals shoulder the heavy responsibility that their leadership affects the learning of students in the school. And they work hard to ensure that teachers in turn own the responsibility of affecting the learning of their students.

Moving into the principal's role is a difficult transition. Or at least I believe it should be a difficult transition. You were probably a highly effective teacher and successful in building relationships with your students and achieving student results. You demonstrated leadership capabilities, and following a promotion, you now are in charge of teachers, who do the job you used to do. It goes without saying that the most important people in your school are the students. But your focus is no longer aimed directly at your students; it is now aimed at your teachers. Your role is now all about leading, supporting, and uniting the teachers for the work of your school. What happens in teachers' classrooms is the most important work. You now are in a position to ultimately affect all students by supporting their teachers. University of Houston professor and best-selling author Brené Brown (2018) writes,

"School leaders have enormous power and influence, and how they use that power and influence changes people. For better or worse" (p. 132).

I know from my own experience the work it takes to succeed as a school leader, and make sure others succeed. I never intended to be an administrator. I truly adored teaching English at the middle and high school levels. But my leadership work in schools led me from being a classroom teacher to guidance counselor to assistant principal. After several years as an assistant, I was placed in the principal's seat at Scribner Middle School in New Albany, Indiana. The nine years I served as principal there are the highlight of my career. Working with that staff—trying to become all we possibly could be—will always hold a special place in my heart. After those meaningful years as principal, I transitioned to the district office to lead all three middle schools in the New Albany Floyd County Consolidated School Corporation. Those were exciting years in aligning the work and creating a true middle school team. I share my experiences from my work in that district throughout this book.

Principals must be aware that they are the essential factor and have enormous power in creating high-achieving schools. And they must also understand what it means to lead. The Indo-European root of the word *lead* is *leit*, which means to go forth—meaning that leaders must be determined to step across the threshold, to step ahead, to go first as a guide (Lead, n.d.). Leaders know the nuts and bolts of the work to be done, but they must also have the spirit of leadership to create a passion in people to get the work done. In other words, principals step out to guide their staff. They go first by using the essential actions and skills necessary for the work ahead. Leaders make the choice to let go of whatever might be limiting their decision to act and intentionally step forward (Hanig & Senge, 2015). Sometimes, the leader may be a bit off-balance with an overwhelming initiative, but she steps ahead and begins the journey anyway. She's courageous in moving forward, stepping out first to pave the way, and bringing others along.

Today's environment demands so much from leaders. Gone are the days when principals served as managers of the building. In today's schools, principals must guide classroom instruction, monitor student learning, oversee school safety, communicate with parents, and create community partnerships. The most successful leaders create a pull toward, not a push against, them. They continuously reflect on their actions and skills with staff members, students, parents, and the community to determine whether they are creating a pushing or pulling style (Levine, 2016). The purpose of this book is to help you understand that successful principals are able to draw people into the real work and accomplish incredible things. But have no doubts; the principal is the essential factor in creating the environment for high-achieving schools.

My life work is in the field of education. For many years of my life my mind was tormented by the thoughts that I need to be doing something else. But God! Who kept me anchored who reminded me of my why in April 2023. I will serve the community of Kankakee with a lit fire now ablaze to advocate for the betterment of the lives of the students, parents, staff and community.

The Deliberate and Courageous Principal

Five Deliberate Actions
Part 1

 Establish a vision focused on learning.

 Clarify the essential work.

 Create teams to move the work forward.

 Take action instead of being busy.

 Lead effective meetings.

Five Courageous Skills
Part 2

 Build relationships.

 Reframe conflict.

 Hold people accountable.

 Lean into the positive.

 Turn inward.

Essential Leadership Actions

I remember it like it was yesterday. It was November 2009, and I was sitting at a banquet table in the downtown Indianapolis Marriott as I was announced as the 2009 Indiana Middle School Principal of the Year. I felt nauseated. I felt like a fraud. I had been a principal for eight years, but I still felt like a fraud. I stood up, my heart pounding fiercely; made the long walk from the back of the banquet room to the stage; and stood behind the podium microphone. On that excruciating walk to the front, two thoughts kept running through my mind: (1) to thank the people back home in my school and district and (2) to not let the audience know I felt like an impostor. I don't remember much once I started speaking. But my closing sentence is singed in my memory forever: "I'm honestly still afraid that everyone's going to figure out I don't know what I'm doing and that I'm just guessing my way through this work of being a principal!"

Yes, I said that. And the audience laughed. I certainly did not mean to say aloud the mixed-up thoughts running around in my head. And I certainly did not expect people to laugh. Perhaps people laughed because they thought I was being humble. Maybe they thought I was trying to be funny, because how could a person become Principal of the Year and not know what she is doing? Ultimately, many principals in the room probably laughed because they felt the same way I did. They also struggled to know exactly what to do as the leader of their school.

After the ceremony, no one mentioned anything to me about my comments, but I have thought about those words quite often over the years. My words were truthful—I meant them—but at the time, I could not figure out *why* I felt like an impostor. My training, principal preparation program, and education courses had been invaluable and meaningful. Yet I still felt at a loss, still felt incompetent. Why?

Overwhelmed with the enormous amount of information from my schooling, I wasn't certain I was concentrating on the right work. This lack of confidence was also a product of my understanding that the work of serving as an effective school principal is extremely difficult and complex. Principals are dealing with human beings, not widgets. Principals are trying to figure out what each student explicitly needs to make learning progress. I knew

I was responsible for this, and I felt like I was guessing at exactly where to start and what to put in place.

Early in my leadership role as a principal, I decided to dig deep into research and experience to find the answers to those questions that kept me up at night. I continued this journey of research into my doctoral thesis in 2014. In this first part of the book, I'll look at five essential leadership actions that I recommend embedding in your school. These are five actions that all principals need to build their competence and lay the groundwork for critical achievement. The five essential leadership actions are:

1. Establish a vision focused on learning

2. Clarify the essential work

3. Create teams to move the work forward

4. Take action instead of being busy

5. Lead effective meetings

Each chapter in part 1 will explore one of these actions. Time to get started.

CHAPTER 1

Establish a Vision Focused on Learning

Visioning is a powerful action that principals often overlook. It may feel like a soft, dreamy aspect of the work that won't make much difference to the school. (Who has time to focus on such a thing?) But creating a vision lays the foundation for everything else. Taking the time to establish a vision is critical for a school's growth. Peter Senge, senior lecturer at the MIT Sloan School of Management and founder of the Society for Organizational Learning, notes that leadership is the capacity to shape the organization's future (as cited in World of Business Ideas, 2012). The vision is the definition of this future in words. It can lead to powerful actions and remarkable results.

This chapter focuses on the intentional work of establishing a vision. We'll focus on foundational questions to define what a vision is, what to know before creating one, why and how to create it, and when to use it. Then the chapter offers some reflection questions and an opportunity to think about next steps. Creating a vision is not a new idea, but truly leading a school with a vision is a rare thing. I urge you to think of this work as creating a vision *story* for your school. You'll be writing a story that will help your staff see a vibrant and exciting picture of their school's future. Some schools will use a few sentences in their vision story; some schools will use a few paragraphs. There isn't an ideal length; it's what feels best to you as the leader. Effective principals ask staff members to do extremely hard work. The least we principals can do is give our staff the professional courtesy of seeing the school's vision, their future, laid out in front of them.

Prior to writing the vision story, you must lead your staff to a clear understanding of the core purpose of your school, the reason for your school's existence, often referred to as the *mission*. Leaders can't move on to establishing a relevant and motivating vision story until they have discussed the school's fundamental purpose.

You can begin this discussion of your school's core purpose with your current leadership team. This discussion will answer the vital question, Why do we exist? along with supporting questions like, Why are we here in our community? and What is the most vital and essential reason for our existence? Take the necessary time to listen to your leadership team's thoughts, ideas, and reasons it feels the school exists in your community. Collaboration with your team is central to this core purpose discussion.

The very first time I did this exercise with my leadership team at Scribner Middle School, it was a really hot day in July. It was our annual off-site meeting day, and this discussion took almost two hours. I remember it well because the lengthy conversation totally messed up the day's agenda. I definitely hadn't allotted enough time for this to be the meaningful dialogue it turned out to be.

Our team members discussed all the things we were doing in our school that we thought were important. We talked about the poverty of our families and the numerous projects we had begun to assist with clothing and food. We talked about our students' needs for after-school activities and the clubs we had established. We talked about all the things we were doing with classroom management so that students would be suspended at lower rates. We talked about our feeder elementary schools and brainstormed strategies for strengthening the rigor of their curriculum so students would achieve at higher levels when they entered our secondary doors. We even discussed how to purchase new cheerleading uniforms!

Finally, we got to the core purpose of our work. We concluded that we were about student learning. We knew that we wanted to become a true professional learning community (PLC) and we knew this core purpose mirrored that of a PLC as developed by Richard and Rebecca DuFour and Robert Eaker, the architects of the PLC at Work® process. The big ideas of a PLC (focus on student learning, collaboration, and results) are what this work—the five actions—is founded upon (DuFour, DuFour, Eaker, Many, & Mattos, 2016). At our school, we had become complacent and allowed our focus to drift away from our instruction and how students were learning. It was time for serious transformation. It was time to build. We needed to build effective, clear lessons, quality assessments so students could demonstrate their understanding, and a schedule that gave us time for true collaboration. We wanted our students learning as much as they possibly could while they attended our school.

The other discussion topics—clothes closet, food assistance, student clubs—were really important, but they should not take us away from our core purpose. We realized we didn't need to spend another minute discussing elementary concerns when we didn't have our own instructional rigor where it needed to be. Each time our discussion led us down another path about something else, we paused. We brought our focus back to student learning and the work we needed to get done. Our purpose was to create an environment of enriching and rigorous instruction and to embed it in our classrooms, where students could enjoy learning. We wanted each of our students to thrive and move forward, making substantial gains in achievement.

I'll be honest. It's easier to talk about the clothes closet, food pantry, after-school clubs, and cheerleading uniforms. When you get to the core purpose, you get down to the difficult and demanding work of aligned, engaging instruction. You get down to establishing processes and having them in place to solidify that students are learning in every classroom. That means teachers would have to change some of their instruction; it means teachers would need to collaborate with other teachers to discuss data and monitor student achievement; and it means teachers would need to incorporate new strategies. Trust me. It was so much easier to stay focused on the after-school tutoring program and family night snack options.

After our July off-site meeting, our leadership team members took our core purpose back to each of the groups they represented for further discussion. After two weeks' time, we met as an entire staff to review our thoughts on this ultimate question of why we exist. We needed our core purpose to be clear and true; we needed our core purpose to help establish our vision. And we needed to become a PLC with a vision. Richard DuFour and Robert Eaker (1998) write that the vision must be "characterized by a consistently high state of urgency and the absence of complacency if [schools] are guided by a compelling picture of a future that is clearly superior to the status quo" (p. 55). We knew we had a lot of work to do, and we didn't want to underestimate the power of our vision.

Although it was a messy conversation at certain points, the entire group came together. We understood we couldn't move on to establishing our vision story until we firmly understood our main reason for existing. This wasn't about making more T-shirts advertising another slogan. We finally understood that we were aligning around our core purpose. We existed to provide our students with aligned, rigorous instruction so they could learn at high levels. We were responsible for providing the time and support they needed to achieve. And we wanted to do it better than any other school.

The leadership team, along with the entire faculty, had answered the question of our existence. We were solely devoted to student learning. We were aware that there was other important work at our school, but none of it was more essential than our instruction as the key factor for student learning. Our purpose, and reason for existence, revolved around creating a school with aligned, rigorous instruction.

When you try this Why Do We Exist? exercise with your leadership team, here are a few responses that could arise from your discussion to help your school's vision focus on learning.

- "We exist to ensure our students have the highest levels of instruction for their learning and to make certain they grow each year."

- "We have high expectations for our students' learning, and we accept our responsibility to help each of them reach those expectations. We will adjust our instructional strategies until we see our students make progress. We will provide immediate, specific, and effective interventions for all students who do not learn an essential concept."

- "We need to provide an aligned curriculum with challenging, high-quality classroom lessons for all our students. We will do that in a caring school environment."

Once you and your staff have a clear answer to your school's core purpose or mission, it's time to move on to the work of establishing a vision. There can be no real impact on the school if the mission simply states that all students can learn or that your school is focused on learning. DuFour and Eaker (1998) write:

> Instead, they must challenge themselves to answer the tougher question that addresses the very heart of the purpose of schooling: What is it we expect our students to learn, and how will we fulfill our collective responsibility to ensure that this learning takes place for all of our students? (p. 62)

Your clear mission, or purpose, lays the foundation for your school's vision, or its future (DuFour et al., 2016).

Reflect on Five Foundational Questions for Establishing a Vision

Principals should take the time to reflect on the following five questions and determine what action steps are necessary to ensure their schools have a clear idea of where they are going and how they're going to get there.

Question 1: What Is a Vision?

A vision is a tool that allows you and your team to define the future of your school in vivid terms. A vision is the first step in planning. It's not what you currently see at your school; it's what you can imagine. It's dreaming together and getting it down on paper. With a vision, you can create a complete picture of what the school's future will look like in two to three years. It helps define the path and identify the things your school needs to accomplish. Visions are not vague dreams. They're not hopeful wishes. Visions can create a clear, specific picture of what the future can hold. With a vision in place, you can create the critical steps of bringing that vision into reality. It can be an invaluable tool to inspire your staff and open them up to new possibilities and to think and operate in a new way.

John Graham (n.d.), author and leader of the global nonprofit Giraffe Heroes Project, writes:

> To create a vision that's exciting and compelling, you've got to give yourself the freedom to dream—to use your imagination to see and feel what does not yet exist. A vision is not the same as goals or objectives; those come from the head. A vision comes from the heart.

I want to be very clear as I talk about a school's vision. I'm not talking about meaningless exercises like our principals had been required to do in the past and that many of you have been asked to do also in your districts. In these exercises, principals were required to complete a template with our vision and other components every few years. I have really negative memories of those experiences. I recall long faculty meetings where we would have lengthy discussions and debates over a single word in our vision statement. Honestly, it took us an entire semester or more to finalize our wording. We often became exasperated and just used any staff suggestions. We eventually sent a long, meaningless document to the district office just to be done with the process. We never could remember what we'd written unless we looked it up. And we certainly never gave the vision much thought until we were required to write it all over again.

Effective principals lead their staff in creating a compelling, energizing, and exciting vision for their school. It's a clear, realistic target of what the school can look like in just a few years.

Question 2: Why Have a Vision?

Consider the following reasons for establishing a vision for your school.

- Even though visions are all about the future, they can energize the present.
- A powerful vision pulls people together with its ideas to create energy around the work that needs to begin in the school.

- A well-written vision inspires people to commit to the work and to persist when things become challenging.

- A precise, inspirational vision can produce change much more effectively than dull, meaningless statements can.

- A vision can provide a clear purpose and serve as a practical guide for setting goals and making decisions. It can lead a school to understand what it must become in order to reach the vision.

- Schools create visions from shared ideas of the work they need to accomplish. From that vision, all staff members should have a clear understanding of their individual goals and relevance in being part of the shared vision.

Once a vision is in place for the school, staff members can see where they're headed. They can see the obstacles and challenges that lie ahead. They can work together toward solutions. The school's vision can turn any team members' fears about the unknowns into confidence. How can a vision do that? Because staff members know explicitly where they're headed; they understand their responsibility; and they trust their school leadership to provide any needed support. If you want to unify your staff into a team that's focused and working together, a vision is your starting point.

Question 3: What Do You Need to Know Before You Create the Vision?

The answers to questions 1 and 2 about what a vision is and why you need a vision should lead you to fully understand that student learning is the reason for your school's existence. But far too often, principals delegate the work of creating clear instructional documents and assessments to other people. Having a systematic, engaging academic core in place is not these principals' number-one priority. An *academic core* refers to the curricular pieces of pacing guides, assessments, data discussions, literacy frameworks, and mathematics frameworks. Even if your school is fortunate enough to have full-time instructional coaches, you as principal, must still be knowledgeable about the curricular pieces. You must know the academic core components; you must know the instructional focus for your departments and grade levels each semester; and you must know the intentional growth area in every subject.

When outside consultants, district instructional coaches, or your school's lead teachers facilitate professional development, you must be in attendance, present, and fully engaged. You should sit down in the front, learn about the instructional strategies, and be involved in discussion with teachers about embedding those strategies into classrooms. This way, your teachers understand that learning and instruction are your most critical concerns. Phil Warrick (2020), Marzano Resources author and associate, firmly believes this, stating, "Effective principals are always in a state of being continuous learners of pedagogy and are always strengthening their knowledge base. The better they are at leading instruction, the better the instruction will be at their school."

I want to stop briefly to answer a question that may have occurred to you by this point: Why is all this information about an academic core located in this chapter about establishing your school's vision? Because far too many times, a school's vision doesn't highlight student learning and teacher instruction. If your teachers are not clear about your priorities and expectations for learning, your vision may not be headed in the right direction. It's worth it to slow down to answer question 3 to make absolutely certain you don't allow things to get muddied. You can leave no room for doubt about the fact that you are communicating a clear vision of your school's purpose and building the beautiful story of your school's vision on the foundation of a solid academic core.

It doesn't take leaders long to understand that there are no magic beans for developing a quick and easy academic core. There are no computer programs that will fix everything. There are no online courses to get students reading at grade level. There are no publishing companies that can get everything in place and provide all the instructional materials in a ready-to-go format. Put simply, there are no easy solutions. Developing an academic core takes a lot of work, and principals must understand how to build and sustain this solid academic core.

The differentiating factor in high-achieving schools is that principals embed these academic components in a deep and systematic way. As soon as one instructional piece is in place and running smoothly, work begins on the next needed action. This process is dynamic, and leaders are relentless in continually examining their practice and looking for ways to improve. It's complex and extremely difficult. That's why so many principals focus on other, easier things or stay busy doing anything but the work of understanding and supporting quality instruction. They delegate this academic core work to teachers and assume everything's taken care of without their involvement. They are abandoning their post and letting others steer the ship.

It is a principal's responsibility to be ready when a parent, teacher, or district leader asks, "Tell me about your curriculum in this particular subject or grade level. What strengths do you see in instruction from individual teachers? Where do your students struggle? What are you doing to support instruction in those areas?"

To answer those questions, you must work with teachers to set strategic and intentional goals around what students will learn in each curricular unit. DuFour and his colleagues (2016) write, "The question 'Learn what?' is one of the most significant questions the members of a PLC will consider. In fact, the entire PLC process is predicated on a deep understanding on the part of all educators of what all students must know and be able to do as a result of every unit of instruction" (p. 113). Be part of this process. School goals, department or grade-level goals, teacher goals, and then student goals are determined from the strategic standards teachers select for their instruction. Give teachers the time and support they need to develop rigorous lessons and units. Then monitor that instruction and continually work to strengthen the core learning in your school. You never take a back seat in this essential work. You, as leader, are continually visible—up front and center—learning, discussing, and embedding each piece of the work.

There are numerous resources to guide you in understanding and developing a solid academic core. I've listed a few that were invaluable to me in developing an academic core in this book's References and Resources section (page 175). *Focus: Elevating the Essentials to Radically Improve Student Learning* (Schmoker, 2011), *A Handbook for High Reliability Schools: The Next Step in School Reform* (Marzano, Warrick, & Simms, 2014), *Leaders of*

Learning: How District, School, and Classroom Leaders Improve Student Achievement (DuFour & Marzano, 2011), *Learning by Doing: A Handbook for Professional Learning Communities at Work* (DuFour et al., 2016), and *Professional Learning Communities at Work: Best Practices for Enhancing Student Achievement* (DuFour & Eaker, 1998) were especially key to my understanding and growth.

One invaluable resource I'll mention here in more detail involves delving into the best practices of building PLCs. In *Learning by Doing*, the authors guide readers' work in answering the four critical questions of a PLC:

> a. What knowledge, skills, and dispositions should every student acquire as a result of this unit, this course, or this grade level?
>
> b. How will we know when each student has acquired the essential knowledge and skills?
>
> c. How will we respond when some students do not learn?
>
> d. How will we extend the learning for students who are already proficient? (DuFour et al., 2016, p. 36)

These four critical questions lay the foundation for the academic core pieces. Building a solid pacing guide answers the first question; creating common formative assessments answers the second question; and developing interventions and accelerations answers the final two questions. Students' academic progress does not primarily depend on demographics and the socioeconomic status of families and the community. What happens within a school with a strong, intentional academic core can highly influence students' progress. Now let's take a brief look at five foundational curricular pieces that make up the academic core: (1) pacing guides, (2) common formative assessments, (3) the literacy framework, (4) the mathematics framework, and (5) units of study.

Pacing Guides

School staff members should view these supportive and helpful documents as a way to provide clarity for teachers and administrators. *Pacing guides* are documents that guide instruction for a certain period of time, usually one quarter, and identify the standards or units to be taught during that time. Teachers create pacing guides to wrap their quality planning and instructional delivery around. In large districts, teachers are often selected from each school to serve on an instructional committee that makes certain all teachers have a voice in the process. You can use them while observing in classrooms as you look for instruction based on the essential targets for that quarter. When grade-level teams or departments meet, pacing guides are part of the discussion. Pacing guides are living, breathing documents— that is, teachers continually revise and improve them to establish a clear instructional path. Pacing guides help teachers and leaders clearly answer the first critical question of a PLC.

Common Formative Assessments

Once the pacing guides are established, teachers also work together to create common formative assessments (CFAs). DuFour and his colleagues (2016) write:

> Using a common assessment means students who are in the same curriculum and are expected to acquire the same knowledge, skills, and dispositions will

be assessed using the same instrument or process, at the same time, or within a very narrow window of time. (p. 134)

These assessments will help answer the second critical question of a PLC: How will we know when each student has acquired the essential knowledge and skills? (DuFour et al., 2016). There are numerous resources about CFAs and the best ways of creating quality assessments to assist in creating the assessments or to strengthen the ones you have. *Common Formative Assessments 2.0* by Larry Ainsworth (2014) and *Embedded Formative Assessment* by Dylan Wiliam (2011) are two of my favorites.

When teachers use these assessments effectively, they help guide instruction in each classroom. Pretests provide valuable information and can assist teachers in knowing specific areas that will need additional support or areas that will require some review during that particular quarter. Posttests and quarterly assessments will show where reteaching needs to occur in the core instruction, and they will show where teachers need to provide acceleration for students needing more time and assistance in understanding the priority content standards. With CFAs embedded in instruction, principals can analyze, along with their teachers, their students' progress and engage in meaningful conversations. They can begin to chart progress student by student, teacher by teacher, and skill by skill. They look at the numbers and they look at student work. These principals know the effect the teachers are having on student learning.

Literacy Framework

In addition to the essential pieces of pacing guides for planning and CFAs for quality assessment, schools must have a clear and systematic *literacy framework* in place. This framework establishes the way reading and writing instruction will occur in the school and throughout the district. Sometimes a literacy framework in grades K–6 will involve a ninety-minute period of instruction with key components of a minilesson, vocabulary work, and guided reading groups.

A literacy framework is not just an elementary school core component; this is an essential piece of middle school and high school academic requirements. The literacy framework cannot stop as students leave the elementary grades. Middle schools must prepare the same aligned framework for students through eighth grade. Middle school English and special education teachers can be trained and proficient in providing guided groups and assistance for students struggling to read at grade level. You must make certain to create effective school schedules in which this extended reading time is available. Extra time embedded in the day must be a priority for those students needing additional support.

For students requiring additional support and time, the literacy framework should continue on to the high school level. Students need to read longer passages and books, analyzing them in greater depth. They should be able to compare multiple texts and determine the credibility of the sources. All principals must be determined to build an aligned, seamless system to make certain their students receive reading assistance.

A literacy framework involves more than reading. It must also involve a systematic approach for writing. You must lead the way in making writing a priority at your school and give it the attention it deserves. Work with teachers to select specific graphic organizers and build rubrics together as part of the framework to ensure that students are reading complex pieces, discussing them deeply in their classrooms, and then writing about them across the curriculum. *Focus* by Mike Schmoker (2011) is an invaluable resource, especially the chapter titled "English Language Arts Made Simple." Lead your staff to understand that proficient writing achievement is not solely the responsibility of English teachers. The entire faculty works together on students' reading complex pieces, discussing them deeply, and then writing analytic essays and supporting their own ideas with evidence.

A middle school science teacher once shared his thoughts on this topic with me and told me that real change for his school came when the English teachers convinced the staff that they were *all* language arts teachers. They were all accountable for teaching students to be literate. They were all accountable for teaching reading, writing, listening, and speaking. He told me it was really tough at first. The science teachers had many times before heard from their administrators that this was their responsibility, but when the message came from fellow teachers asking for help, it got through to them. They listened to their colleagues. The English teachers taught specific strategies to the science teachers for them to incorporate in their science instruction. They assisted the science teachers in selecting better texts for their science units. He commented to me several times that this process wasn't easy, but once the staff saw their students achieving at much higher levels, they didn't need convincing anymore. Every department, not just science, began having its students read more complex texts, discuss things more deeply than what was readily obvious in the pieces, and then write about their findings. He told me he couldn't remember anything else making such an impact on his school.

Mathematics Framework

Just as a literacy framework is essential in an academic core, a mathematics framework is as well. Along with the mathematics pacing guide and common formative assessments, mathematics teachers need a system in place for components like daily mathematics review, conceptual teaching, and problem solving.

I was extremely moved when I visited a high school where problem solving was a critical focus throughout its mathematics department. The teachers wanted their students to solve problems—really tough problems. One day every other week was devoted to solving such problems. Students received a difficult mathematics problem to solve, usually requiring numerous mathematical steps. Students began by trying to solve the problem on their own. Then teachers placed them in small groups to work together. The students received time to review what other groups had done before finalizing their answer. Teachers served as guides for this activity, building students' perseverance in trying to reach a solution. Instead of quickly providing answers or the next step to take, teachers would intentionally give clues to nudge students who were struggling. In essence the teachers gave as little assistance as they could—but always enough to motivate their students to push ahead in the process. Once student groups shared their work, the teachers spent time reviewing the correct ways of solving the problem. Usually, there were at least a couple of ways. No more one right answer. If students had made mistakes, teachers were quick to clear up any misunderstandings and allowed other students to share how they had arrived at the correct answer. Therefore, when the state assessment arrived and required problem solving, this was not new to students. Problem solving was a consistent part of their mathematics experience throughout the year.

In another district, I was surprised at the depth of discussion in one middle school seventh-grade mathematics team's meetings. Team members were focused on alignment. Really focused. If they didn't introduce a mathematics concept at their grade level, they invited teachers from the prior grade level to explain how they introduced the concept and how much they were able to accomplish with students. One example that stands out is a discussion on slope. Students were struggling to understand and become proficient on this concept. Even though the skill was introduced in sixth grade, these seventh-grade teachers were breaking apart the students' work and seeing where the confusion was coming. Sometimes, these conversations made it clear to the current grade-level teachers that they needed to review the concept and introduce it again. They also realized that they needed to be using the same vocabulary and mathematical language for the same concept from grade to grade. Otherwise, they would confuse students.

Teachers in these two schools were consistently asking their principals for more time to meet together. You can see why—they had a system in place. The teacher team members met for fifty minutes before school once a week and for a forty-five-minute planning period during the school day each week. They filled those minutes with the work discussed previously. The evidence was clear. These teachers wanted to make their instruction as effective as they possibly could. Their laser-like focus and meticulous work clearly exemplified this.

One of the middle school teachers shared with me that it was difficult not to work on every concept on which students were struggling. She reported that she and her team members came to understand they never really fixed anything if they tried to fix everything. Once they chose one specific skill, they worked together until they found a better instructional way. They were determined to help students make gains. They were determined to address the issue so that it did not repeat itself every year. Next quarter, they moved on to a new concept. Their plan was to eventually refine all skills and concepts; they just had to teach themselves first. It was really hard work, but they were certainly doing it. They were establishing, through intensive collaboration, a mathematics framework for their school.

Units of Study

Most schools require teachers to be involved in the work of creating a pacing guide for their particular subject. At some schools, teachers then determine the number of units per quarter, usually two or three, and begin developing units based on one or two standards.

There are several methods for unit development. Problem-based learning and rigorous curriculum design are just two examples. *Problem-based learning* incorporates real-world problems as a vehicle to engage students in their learning. This approach is obviously much better than rote presentations of facts and concepts. *Rigorous curriculum design* also keeps students at the center of its lessons. There are precise learning targets, engaging classroom experiences, and multiple opportunities for students to show their knowledge. Most unit-development methods have unit elements in common, including an engaging scenario for the launching of the unit, rigorous activities, complex reading, writing requirements, and a culminating project or assessment.

I worked with a middle school principal whose teachers would meet as departments or grade levels to share their thoughts on how well the units worked. But the principal and teachers also met with students for feedback. They asked students questions like, "What was the best part of this unit for you? How could we make the unit better and more interesting? Did we give you enough time to be creative and innovative in the way you were asked to show your knowledge of the material? Do you have any ideas to share with us that could enrich the unit? Would you rank these unit activities according to their relevance for you and the amount of deep thinking required?" Teachers not only asked these questions but also listened to the responses. Then they worked together on revisions and enhancements for the units. As a result, students seemed to be truly engaged in their learning.

These unit frameworks were invaluable tools for that principal to use as he made classroom visits and met with departments for curricular discussions. He even displayed the unit frameworks in the front office so that parents and community members could see a clear picture of what students were learning at that particular point in the year.

In summarizing the academic core, I'll share this final thought. Principals can easily say, "Sure, we have pacing guides, common formative assessments, and units of study. Yes, we've already got a solid academic core in place. Now what?" But I urge you to look closely at the academic core pieces at your school. Don't just check these items off your list and move on. Make certain you see deep and thoughtful instruction, debate for bettering that instruction, and refinement of each piece of the teaching.

I realize that building a solid academic core represents a persistent commitment to getting better. It's much easier to initiate change than to consistently keep pushing that change forward once the process has begun. But if you continue to work each day on the pieces of your academic core, you should see a strong, solid academic core in place in less than two years. As journalist and author James Clear (n.d.b), who specializes in creating good habits, writes, "Rome wasn't built in a day, but they were laying bricks every hour."

Remember, establishing an academic core is the work of high-achieving schools. They keep moving forward to strengthen the instructional system. High-achieving principals are effective at guiding this work. They continue nudging things forward, week by week, and leading through the difficult times.

Question 4: How Do You Create Your School's Vision?

To create the vision, you must first take a hard look at the current state of things in your school. Make a list of all the positive and negative aspects that you need to address. Usually, the vision starts to become clear with the priority items that move to the top of the list. And often, you'll realize that in order for the prioritized work to get accomplished, staff members will need to stop doing some of their current work requirements.

Leaders must have an organized way to determine what the school needs to stop doing so the necessary time is available for future initiatives. Organized abandonment serves this purpose. Peter Drucker, a renowned management consultant, teaches that organizations need to free up the resources that don't contribute any longer to getting results (as cited in Rutherford Learning Group, n.d.). In schools, principals must continually assess and identify things that can be abandoned so that teachers can have the needed time and resources for the new tasks.

When teachers are clear on what their leaders expect, they can then abandon the nonessential activities in order to have time for the critical, rigorous work. Consider organized abandonment as creating your stop-doing list and having teachers check off items on the list. Free up resources, evaluate everything, and lead staff to the essential work. It's not that teachers are not doing enough; rather, they're trying to do too much and struggling to do it all well. The goal is not about how many tasks teachers can tackle; it's about the tasks teachers can let go of in order to really excel in their instruction.

You might try thinking of your school as a garden, a cultivated, living system. Gardens are always growing something new right beside the plants that have taken root. Principals determine the current initiatives, the perennial plants, that are worthy of existence and then prepare the list of new initiatives the school needs, the new seedlings. Getting the right, rigorous initiatives in place is like growing the new plants amid the solid, flowering plants that already exist. And, of course, it involves helping staff understand the work that can be pruned back and totally removed from the garden. It's your job to guide this balance—beginning a few initiatives, maintaining the important ones, and letting go of a few unworthy ones.

Now, take the list of prioritized work and move to get the vision out of your head and into written form. I've found that using adjectives, numbers, pictures, and stories helps in describing the vision. You might start by sharing stories of what you envision for the school in one or two years. Your stories could describe what you hope for other school districts to see should they visit your school; these descriptions could include how your aligned academic core will work or how students will make amazing reading gains each year. Then add specific adjectives, and phrases to describe the school in your vision—like *aligned, efficient, accountable,* or *whatever it takes.* You can also include numbers to show the percentage of growth in students' academic priorities, like eighth-grade problem solving moving from 66 percent of students achieving proficiency on the state assessment to 80 percent achieving proficiency. Or numbers can show student engagement with enrichment programs, like the specific number of students enrolled in the International Baccalaureate program increasing from thirty-two to fifty. Numbers can address disciplinary concerns, like reducing the percentage of students receiving out-of-school suspension from 20 percent to 10 percent. By using pictures, adjectives, numbers, and stories to specifically describe what the school could look like in just a few years, the principal can create a compelling vision for all staff members.

Next, share your vision with the school's leadership team so members can listen, ask questions, and add their thoughts and ideas. Your vision is the starting point; the team's vision is the ending point. By facilitating a rich discussion with the team, you, the leader, can strengthen and build on the vision. Adding in these contributions from key staff members will create more buy-in. Dream about the future together. Give your team permission to think about the next few years. Create conditions for your team to talk about the future and all the possibilities for your school. Conduct informal hallway and lunch conversations together.

Our vision story went something like this in that first year at Scribner Middle School: We must create rigorous and intentional instruction for each grade level and department each quarter. We must also create assessments so we will know what our students understand after our instruction. Time for student interventions will be placed in the daily schedule this year. Time for teachers to meet together will be placed in the daily schedule this year. We will take full responsibility for our students' learning. We will no longer settle for mediocre proficiency scores in mathematics and English language arts. We will work together—in our teams with real data conversations—to achieve 70 percent proficiency levels in both subjects. Our district office and surrounding schools will begin making visits to our school to see all the amazing work and success taking place!

The goal is to create a shared vision with staff. You don't want to simply tell staff members what the vision is. You want to develop the vision together. "It's a bit paradoxical. The vision is a whole, but the individuals see that vision from their points of view and then act in ways to bring about the whole" (Hanig & Senge, 2015). Staff members need to understand their specific relevance and their individual work are critical to the school as a whole. Then motivation and inspiration can well up within each educator to get those things accomplished.

After the leadership team has completed its work of listening, sharing, and revising, the principal then shares the updated vision with the entire staff, encouraging everyone to offer feedback. Even though the principal may stick to the vision finalized with the leadership team, everyone's participation and contributions create more ownership and can make implementation easier. Don't allow this process to get bogged down. You can move from your original vision to a shared school vision in two to three weeks.

I'm hesitant to share examples of school vision stories because it's important that each school establish its own unique vision for its specific needs. But here's a sample middle school vision story to give you an idea:

> Our school is a standout in our community. We have more transfer requests than we've ever had in the history of our school. We can't even accept all of the families wanting their kids to attend our school. Our students are achieving at the highest levels ever. Students reading at grade level at the end of their eighth-grade year have increased from 72 percent to 85 percent. Our rigorous literacy alignment has paid off! Our students want to be here; student attendance has grown from an 88 percent daily rate to 95 percent over the last two years. Our staff is made up of dedicated, data-driven, focused teacher teams doing intentional work of creating engaging, rigorous lessons. There's a new feeling here at [our school]. It's a fresh, inviting, and exciting place to be. Our instructional assistants have been a primary part of our professional development trainings and are an integral piece in our students' achievement. Each and every staff member really does believe they have the power to affect students' lives. Each of us accepts responsibility for our students' achievement. Several schools from across the state are making visits to our school to see and discuss the changes

we've made in our instructional strategies the last two years. We enjoy sharing our success, but they haven't seen anything yet!

Question 5: When Do You Utilize the Vision?

Each year, the work of creating or revising the vision is part of principals' back-to-school work. Bring out your vision from the previous year, review it, revise it, and prepare your updated version for the leadership team. Some leadership teams even begin discussing and revising the vision at the end of the current year, in May or June.

Once you've thought through the process of revisions with the team, you're ready to share the vision with the full staff on the opening staff day. Throughout the year, remind teachers of the vision and of the fact that their work should continually focus on helping the school reach that vision. Bring it up in department and grade-level meetings, in individual teacher conversations, and in the January faculty meeting of each year. The January faculty meeting is a perfect time to discuss achievements from the first semester and focus in on the work for the upcoming semester. If teachers know exactly where they're heading and what that looks like, it can motivate them to find their individual role in bringing the shared vision to reality.

Stand Firm as a Visionary Leader

As this chapter on establishing a vision comes to a close, there's one last thing for me to mention: Being a visionary leader is not easy. The most difficult part is staying true to the vision. Principals should be prepared to hold the tension between the newly created vision and the school's current reality. When a lofty vision is present, some staff members will dig in their heels to cling to old mindsets and negativity. Leaders can use this as an opportunity to inspire people to see beyond their limited thinking. But holding the vision high in cases like this is really tough. It's much easier to compromise the vision and lower expectations than to hold people accountable to them. Through these difficult stages of the work, continue to support your staff. You, as a visionary leader, must stand firm and lead people through the demanding times to move the current reality up to the higher level of the vision. Stay true to the shared vision. Resist the impulses to lower the vision. Hold the tension between the vision and the current reality.

Remember, a vision does several things for the people who work in your school: it creates a deep sense of purpose, it provides motivation, and it establishes a sense of urgency to accomplish the work. Keep your head high and your feet on the ground. Hold the tension, and keep moving forward toward your school's shared vision.

To reflect on creating a school vision and begin work on your next steps, see the reproducible tools on pages 25–27.

Establish Your School's Vision

Take a few minutes to reflect on the following prompts based on the five foundational questions for establishing a vision. Circle the appropriate number rating for each reflection question, with 1 being low, signifying that work is really needed here and 5 being high, signifying that no work is needed. Then write down ideas for improving your work related to each foundational question.

Question and Rating	Notes for Improvement
Question 1: What is a vision? Can I share my understanding of what a vision is and the impact it can have on my school? 1 2 3 4 5	
Question 2: Why have a vision? Am I able to verbalize the why of establishing a shared school vision? 1 2 3 4 5	
Question 3: What do you need to know before you create the vision? What is the current condition of the school's academic core? What are some steps that I know need to be immediately addressed? 1 2 3 4 5	
Question 4: How do you create your school's vision? Have I determined my next steps for establishing a vision for the school? 1 2 3 4 5	
Question 5: When do you utilize the vision? Once the vision is established, do I utilize it in meaningful ways? 1 2 3 4 5	

Academic Core Reflection Questions and Strategies

Take a few minutes to reflect on the following questions based on the five foundational curricular pieces of an academic core. Then list some strategies you can employ to strengthen each component of the academic core.

Academic Core Reflection Questions	Strategies for Strengthening
Pacing Guides • Is a common pacing guide in place for each grade level, department, or course? • Do I use the pacing guide in observations and conversations with teachers? • Do I work with teams to review the document, revise it, and keep it timely and meaningful?	
Common Formative Assessments • Are CFAs in place so that I, along with teachers, understand how students are learning? • Do we have meaningful data conversations after a CFA is administered? • Do I lead teachers in creating instructional goals? Are accelerations and enrichments in place based on the data?	
Literacy Framework • Does the school have a systematic literacy framework in place for all students? Are we aligned in our minilessons, vocabulary work, and guided group instruction? • For students not reading at grade level, does the schedule provide additional time with specific reading strategies in place? • Do teachers monitor reading growth? • Are students consistently reading, discussing, and writing throughout the semester? • Do teachers share students' writing samples with me? With each other? With other students?	
Mathematics Framework • Does the school have a systematic mathematics framework in place for all students? (For example, all mathematics classes begin with a daily mathematics review, all classes have consistent conceptual lessons, all classes have problem-solving posters in place for depth of learning, and so on.) • Do I lead teachers in creating instructional goals? Are accelerations and enrichments in place based on the data?	
Units of Study • Have teachers developed the essential standards into challenging and engaging units for students? • Does each unit have a culminating assessment or project to assess student learning? • Are the units full of interesting texts and writing prompts? • Do I lead teachers in creating instructional goals?	

Vision Brainstorming Template

Now that you've spent some time reflecting on the current state of your school's vision and academic core, use the following template to brainstorm your own ideas for making your school's vision more inspiring and energetic. You can also use it in a brainstorming session with your leadership team.

Date: Name:
A *vision* is a tool that allows you and your staff to define the future of your school in vivid terms. It helps define the path for continuing rigorous, effective practices and identifying things your school needs to accomplish. A vision creates a clear, specific, compelling, and motivating picture of the school in two to three years. When establishing a vision, use your heart and dream big!
Choose adjectives and phrases that clearly describe the school and staff in two to three years.
Determine school, department, and grade-level goals with specific numbers and percentages of achievement gains.
Think of stories that describe in detail what's happening at your school in just two to three years.
Jot down picture ideas or actually sketch a few to illustrate what things in your school look like in two to three years.
Write several sentences incorporating all your preceding thoughts to get a sense of your school's vision for the next two to three years.

CHAPTER 2

Clarify the Essential Work

Now that you've established a shared vision for your school, these questions might be running through your mind.

- "Our school has a shared vision. Now what do I do?"

- "How do I even start to make this vision become a reality?"

- "With so much work to do, where do I begin?"

- "How do I guide staff members toward their individual responsibilities in this work?"

Clarifying the essential work is the leadership action that will help you answer these questions. In this chapter, I will examine three things that can assist you in moving your school forward in achieving your vision. I'll start with the importance of understanding why you must provide clarity for your staff. Then I'll discuss an exercise to help you create a comprehensive inventory of the important work of your school. Finally, I'll introduce a tool to help you prioritize and clarify the critical work, semester by semester. I can't begin this chapter without mentioning a phrase that Becky DuFour, coauthor of twelve books on the topic of professional learning communities, often used in her keynote presentations and writing: "Clarity precedes competence" (Schmoker, 2004, p. 85).

Understand That Clarity Is Essential

At this critical juncture—when the vision is established and the work begins—principals' most significant responsibility is to provide clarity for the work ahead. Simply put, clarity means minimal confusion. Author and business consultant Marcus Buckingham (2005) writes that clarity is "the antidote to anxiety, and that clarity is the preoccupation of the effective leader. If you do nothing else as a leader, be clear" (p. 146). To keep their schools heading in the right direction, school leaders must provide focus and clarity.

Leaders need to understand that their behavior matters and they do have control over the future of their schools. As you begin to provide clarity for your staff, you may find it helpful to consider a powerful metaphor called the Zorro Circle, which appears in author and speaker Shawn Achor's (2011) book *The Happiness Advantage: The Seven Principles That*

Fuel Success and Performance at Work. Achor (2011) shares the story of the fictional masked vigilante Zorro—named Alejandro—who was trained in his early life by Don Diego. Don Diego's goal was to focus the young boy and help him become successful in small things before moving on to larger tasks. Don Diego would draw a small circle on the ground. He would instruct Alejandro to fight only inside that circle. Once he became competent in that particular area, Don Diego would increase the size of the circle and allow Alejandro to compete in the larger space. Eventually and systematically, Alejandro became the magnificent warrior known as Zorro.

As a new principal, I felt overwhelmed with no clear picture of how to handle all the work. Very quickly, I learned there was so much to get done at our school, and I needed to give my full attention to that rather than to district and state responsibilities. I needed to focus on the things that were in my control as the leader of the school. I needed to make my circle smaller. I needed "to regain control by focusing first on small, manageable goals, and then gradually expanding [the] circle to achieve bigger and bigger ones" (Achor, 2011, p. 17). The idea of the Zorro Circle helped me narrow my focus and bring much more clarity to my leadership.

As a leader, you must learn to begin your work in the small circles that are in your control. Once this work of analyzing the curricular frameworks and assessments begins, you will quickly understand that the next steps can be complex and difficult. But if you stay focused within your small circle, and work hard until that work has been successfully completed, then you can move on to the next area of focus—a larger circle—and systematically advance from one success to the next. For example, at Scribner, we started with the revision of our pacing guides to clarify exactly what our teachers wanted students to learn each quarter. Next, we began developing a few simple common assessments to gain an understanding of how the instruction was working. It's a step-by-step process, enlarging the circle with each step.

It's easy for school leaders to spend entirely too much time thinking about the problems *out there* instead of the ones right inside their own school. Effective principals don't sit and wait for answers from the district office; they don't sit and blame the state or province for requirements and mandates; and they don't make excuses for why they can't get initiatives going at their school. Don't waste time on things beyond your control. Focus on the critical and difficult work for which every principal should be held accountable: the work of answering the ultimate question, How are students learning and achieving in our school?

In the book *That's Outside My Boat*, veteran television announcer Charlie Jones tells the story of when he was getting ready to report on the 1996 Olympic Games in Atlanta (Jones & Doren, 2001). He felt incredibly disappointed when he was assigned to broadcast the rowing, canoeing, and kayaking events. In previous years, he had been assigned to witness the excitement of track and field, swimming, and diving. He had reported on the amazing feats of track athlete Florence "Flo-Jo" Griffith Joyner in the 1988 Seoul Games and swimmer Pablo Morales in the 1992 Barcelona Games.

When he arrived in Atlanta a week before the Games, he began interviewing Olympic rowers from all over the world. He asked them the basic question, "What if it's raining?"

The answer would always be, "That's outside my boat." Then he would ask, "What if the wind blows you off course?" The reply would be, "That's outside my boat." What if one of your oars breaks?" "That's outside my boat."

By the end of those Atlanta Games, he reports, they were by far the best of his life. Why? Because he learned so much. He learned invaluable lessons. He came to understand that those Olympic rowers were only interested in and focused on what they could control. They let the outside circumstances go. The rowers knew they had to dismiss the extraneous factors and concentrate all their focus and talent on what was inside their boat. Other reporters also questioned the teams about the rain, the heavy winds, the possibility of broken oars, and other negative aspects. But each team member consistently responded, "That's outside my boat." It's another way of saying that the teams only concentrated on what was inside their circle of influence. They were determined not to waste any mental energy on things that could distract them from the real work they had to do.

Jones writes:

> It slowly began to dawn on me that my assignment was "outside my boat." Dick Ebersol, then president of NBC Sports, hadn't called and asked me what I would like to cover; he had simply given me this venue. What I did with it was up to me. (Jones & Doren, 2001, p. xvii)

Keep your focus and full attention inside your boat, your school. Try not to become distracted by things that aren't in your control. Your school is a precious venue ready to be steered in the right direction with your leadership. What you do within the walls of your school is up to you. But effective leaders clarify the work that needs to get done. They focus on specific areas until those are embedded and strong before moving to the next areas of work. These principals are building a solid base for continued achievement.

Create a Systems List of the Important Work of Your School

Once you understand how essential clarity is, it's time to create a comprehensive list of all the work of your school. This involves the work that is currently going on, the work that needs to begin, and the work that could be discontinued. Only when you have created this comprehensive inventory can the most essential work rise to the top of the list and be prioritized. From our learning in chapter 1 (page 11), you should clearly understand that the most essential work revolves around student learning and teacher instruction. That work of building your academic core will always remain on your list so you can enhance and strengthen each piece.

An exercise I find extremely helpful for creating this comprehensive list resembles the Strategy Amoeba exercise featured in Patrick Lencioni's (2012) book *The Advantage: Why Organizational Health Trumps Everything Else in Business*. I adapted the exercise to fit our needs at Scribner Middle School. With your leadership team, create an exhaustive list of all the things your school needs to do in order to be successful. Make the list as inclusive as you can. Try to think of everything that could possibly go on the list. Of course, you as principal would begin by writing *learning and instruction* as the first item. Then you can add all the other topics.

When my leadership team did this exercise, we put several pieces of chart paper up on the wall. Everyone had a colored marker. After I began with the first item of *learning and instruction*, other team members added topics like *aligning our curriculum, writing units of study, using common formative assessments, providing acceleration and enrichment,* and *collaborating in grade levels and departments.* Then team members broke off from that category of *learning and instruction* and began listing all kinds of things. They added topics like *interviewing new teachers better, creating an induction program for new teachers, making our evaluation system more meaningful,* and so on, and on, and on. Our chart paper was covered with nearly eighty items (see figure 2.1 to see what one portion looked like).

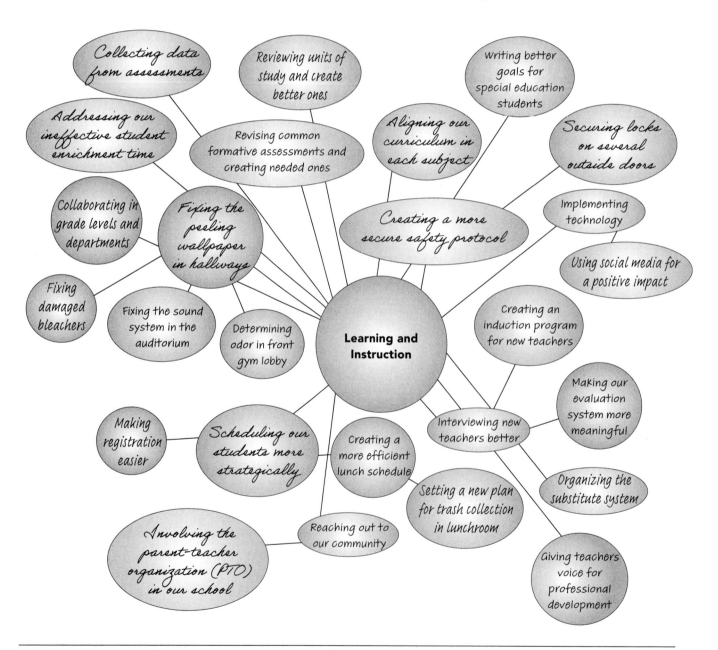

Figure 2.1: A sampling of topics from a comprehensive list.

Once we were finished writing everything we could think of on the chart paper, it truly began to look like a huge amoeba: one big blob, encompassing all kinds of items. Next, we began to place items into categories if they fit together. We made categories on another chart paper and started putting each item under the most accurate category. See the example in figure 2.2 for how we did this for two categories.

Student Learning and Instruction
- *Align the curriculum in each subject.*
- *Review units and create better ones.*
- *Revise common assessments and create needed ones.*
- *Address our ineffective student enrichment time.*

Facilities
- *Fix damaged bleachers.*
- *Determine how to fix the odor in front gym lobby.*
- *Secure the locks on several outside doors.*
- *Fix the peeling wallpaper in hallways.*
- *Set up a new plan for trash collection in lunchroom.*
- *Fix the sound system in the auditorium.*

Figure 2.2: Breaking the comprehensive list into categories.

Items that didn't fit into categories were placed on our list as stand-alone items. For example, no other items fit with the items for student registration and PTO involvement, so they became categories of their own. By the time we had categorized everything, cleaned out the redundant items, and made a final list, we had nearly forty categories of systems on our list. We called the list our *systems list* (see figure 2.3, page 34). (I will discuss this systems list in more detail in chapter 4, page 65.)

Think for a moment about the number of decisions principals make each day. Sometimes it simply feels overwhelming. That's when these systems come into play. When you build and embed your systems, there are fewer decisions to make because the questions have been answered through your systems. There's no need to make decisions time and time again.

- Academic core (continual strengthening of instruction in each subject and grade level for a guaranteed and viable curriculum, including assessment, grading, and homework practices)
- Anti-racism initiatives (curriculum, discipline, and student placement)
- Assembly procedures
- Assessments (national, state, district, and school assessments)
- Athletics and extracurriculars
- Cafeteria procedures for breakfast and lunch
- Classroom management
- Closing day awards program
- Closing-of-school procedures
- Communication system (weekly memo, morning announcements, and so on)
- Community outreach and engagement
- Data collection process and data-driven conversations
- Dual language program
- English learner placement and program
- Facilities
- Finances and budget
- High-ability placement process and requests for removal from program
- Highly effective teacher process for opportunities to strengthen the school
- Induction of new students to the building *during the year*
- Interviewing, hiring, and induction program for new teachers
- Noncertified personnel system for success (including instructional assistants, health aide, front office staff, bookkeeper, school resource officer, cafeteria staff, bus drivers, plant operator, and so on)
- Opening days with teachers
- Opening-of-school procedures (registration, bus procedures, staff duties, and so on)
- Parent-teacher night (open house)
- Parent-teacher organization
- Parent-teacher or student-led conferencing
- PreK system and day care relationships
- Schedules (two-hour delay schedule, early dismissal schedule, morning collaboration schedule, guidance schedule, monthly faculty meetings schedule, and so on)
- School safety and security
- Schoolwide behavior model
- Six meetings of leadership (see chapter 5, page 83)
- Social-emotional system for staff well-being
- Social-emotional system for student well-being
- Social media expectations of staff
- Special education procedures (including Section 504)
- Staff personal- and sick-day procedures
- Strategic scheduling for students and staff
- Student transfer requests (within and without district requests)
- Substitute teachers
- Teacher improvement plan process
- Teacher observations and evaluation conversations
- Technology initiatives and virtual learning
- Transitions *from* elementary school and transitions *to* high school

Figure 2.3: Systems list.

When principals realize there is a need for a system, they build it. And in building the systems, they build clarity. This means less confusion for everyone. Some of the systems are much larger than others and require more work to develop thoroughly. For instance, in my case, the systems of assembly procedures and closing day awards program didn't take too long to review, revise, and strengthen. But systems like the schoolwide behavior model and teacher observations and evaluation conversations took much more time; we had to review the current processes in place, research for better techniques, and determine ways to strengthen those systems. And, as always, the academic core remained at the top of the list for continual work to strengthen our instruction and student learning.

Why do this exercise? First, the leadership team can cohesively work through it together. Each member has a voice. Second, it gives you, as the principal, an introductory activity for providing clarity for your staff; the work of conceiving and organizing a clear, although messy, chart of things our school should be doing really helped everyone see all the systems and pieces that would need to be in place.

Prioritize and Clarify Each Semester's Critical Work

Your school has a shared vision. You've created a systems list of items that need to be in place for your school to succeed. And now it's time to prioritize and clarify that work.

If your school is bursting at the seams with loads of nonessential projects, unimportant work, and cumbersome documents, it won't have time for the critical initiatives. When you, as the leader, are clear about the work to do in the upcoming semester, it becomes easier for you to say no to the nonessentials. Clarity empowers people to get the essential work done. Brown (2018) puts it best: when it comes to this essential clarifying skill of leaders, she writes, "Clear is kind. Unclear is unkind" (p. 48).

How do effective principals create clear, manageable priorities for the school? The tool that I have found most helpful in organizing the work and keeping it alive in a simple format is the principal playbook (adapted from the playbook idea in *The Advantage* [Lencioni, 2012, pp. 134–135]). Let's take a look at five questions that will help you understand this organizational tool.

Question 1: What Is a Principal Playbook?

A principal playbook is a simple, concise document that you create each semester that you customize to your school's specific needs for that semester. It's a tool that helps you concentrate your efforts on specific, reachable, short-term goals. Now that you've established your school's vision, considered the state of your academic core, and determined your systems list, this playbook will help you organize these items for making the vision become a reality. The principal playbook will allow you, semester by semester, to organize a few carefully selected goals to move the essential work forward.

When creating your playbook, you can list each selected area of work in bold at the top of a separate page. After trying several options, I found the best format consisted of four pages with work in these areas.

1. ELA and literacy (reading and writing)

2. Mathematics

3. Other subjects

4. Other systems

These page titles don't require much explanation. With all the accountability of schools to achieve at certain levels in specific subjects, ELA and mathematics are definitely a focus for most schools. Our school certainly had an inordinate amount of work to do in those areas.

As you think about your school's reason for existence and your created vision, it's time to prioritize and set goals for your school's academic core needs (the components of which we discussed in chapter 1, page 11). You, as the instructional leader, must do the work of determining which pieces are well established and embedded, which pieces need tweaking, which pieces need extensive work, and which pieces are not even developed yet. The principal playbook is a key tool to help you do that. I will refer to it again many times throughout this book.

The *ELA* and *mathematics* pages of the principal playbook will give you a specific space to prioritize the work that needs to be done in those subject areas each semester. Principals must lead the work of continually drilling down into and improving instruction in English and mathematics. Then other work continues with specific goals on the *other subjects* page. This page keeps track of the specific instructional goals of all other departments, like social studies, science, art, music, other electives, and so on. Each department and subject area should be continually working toward clear, detailed, and rigorous learning outcomes. Why are three out of four pages dedicated to curricular areas? Because those represent the work of the academic core, the system at the very top of the systems list. This work is the reason schools exist. Students' learning is the most important and the most essential work. As educational leaders, we must make it clear that nothing comes before student learning and teacher instruction. These pages give you a place to develop goals. You may need to begin with basic goals of creating or revising your pacing guides, creating or revising common formative assessments, or determining a guided reading model to utilize in your school. When you have accomplished these goals, you may consider semester work on grading collaboratively on student writing pieces, strengthening data analysis conversations after CFAs, or developing cross-disciplinary writing activities.

The final page, *other systems*, includes goals for setting up all the items on your systems list that need to be addressed. (As a reminder, systems include things like safety, facility needs, opening day, hiring and interviewing, new teacher induction, evaluation and coaching, health office procedures, and so on.)

Each page has a simple template with these columns: Who, What, By When, and Metric. The Metric column simply mentions a measurement tool that will prove the work has been completed. For example, if you have determined to develop your new teacher induction system, you might include something like this: Principal Megan (Who) will bring a copy of the current new teacher induction items (What) to our next meeting on Monday (By When). And when Principal Megan brings those items on Monday and presents them to the group, there's your proof (Metric). After reviewing your current system, you'll determine the next steps. Figure 2.4 shows a blank template for the ELA page in the principal playbook (specific examples for each page appear later in this chapter).

Who	What	By When	Metric

Figure 2.4: Principal playbook page template.

*Visit **go.SolutionTree.com/leadership** for a free reproducible version of this figure.*

Question 2: Why Is a Principal Playbook So Critical?

The principal playbook became the most vital document I used in making our school's work clear and in driving that work forward. Each page had essential goals for ELA, mathematics, other subjects, and other systems. It was a living, breathing document that helped me prioritize and clarify the most important work to focus on in the upcoming semester. That is, I didn't file it away or place it in a desk drawer to be ignored. Once teachers understood the goals for the department or grade level, I asked them to set their individual teaching goals based on the goals of the principal playbook.

The ultimate goal of the principal playbook is to bring clarity to the semester's upcoming work. This principal playbook is for the principal's use. As principal, you discuss all the possible goals with your leadership team so they can help you determine the highest priorities for the upcoming semester. Then you can share the selected goals on each page with your teachers and staff members so they are clear on what you expect. When teachers see the prioritized goals of the school, most often they will be able to determine their own semester goals because they are clear on what they need to accomplish. For example, if you've set a goal for all English teachers in the building to understand the guided group instructional model and to begin using one particular strategy from the model, then the English teachers will know they need to accomplish these things and can set their own individual goals for the semester. Another example might be that you've set a goal for all mathematics teachers to incorporate daily mathematics review in their mathematics instruction each day. Many teachers will select this to be their goal for the upcoming semester: incorporating daily mathematics review and making certain to incorporate all aspects of that strategy.

Principals aren't the only leaders using playbooks. Al Everett (2018), a businessman and former football player, writes about how National Football League teams keep a playbook filled with all the team's most critical information. Each player is expected to know his part of the playbook inside and out so that the team can work together effectively. Each player obviously has the talent and skills to be a member of a professional team, but if each player doesn't know his playbook responsibilities and deliver on them, he isn't doing his part to make the individual football players come together as a team.

The playbook is valuable to the franchise throughout the season, but it's especially so in preseason while players are trying out for the team. If a player loses his copy, he is fined over ten thousand dollars to get a replacement copy. And if things aren't going well with a player's performance, an assistant coach might tell a player, "Coach wants to see you. Bring your playbook." And over time, if the head coach is not happy with a player's overall performance, he will send an assistant coach to the player's room late at night. That visit means the player will no longer be a member of the NFL team. The visit is done late at night so as not to embarrass the player and to allow the player to pack up and be gone before morning (Everett, 2018).

What one item does the assistant coach require from the player before he leaves the team? What item has such importance that the assistant must return it to the head coach first thing the following morning? The playbook. So much work, so many strategies, and so much organizational wealth have gone into that playbook, and it certainly needs to be ready for the next player coming on board (Everett, 2018).

Playbooks can be invaluable for any organization. Everett (2018) suggests that "one of the primary benefits of a purposeful playbook is that it makes iterating and continuous improvement possible." Get your semester goals in place, and get ready to take action. Past experience has shown me that far too often, educators create goals in fancy documents with lots of complex language. Then nothing much happens. Or they start out well, but as soon as they hit some difficulty, the system breaks down, and they're not able to accomplish much. The principal playbook can be a practical and useful tool in simplifying the process of accomplishing the exact things that need to be done in your school.

Working with a school district in 2020, I had introduced the idea of incorporating a principal playbook into its practice. The superintendent wanted principals to use the tool so he would be clear on the focused work happening at each of the schools in his district. He asked the principals to schedule an appointment to present their principal playbooks to the curriculum director and him at the beginning of each semester. Six months after introducing the principal playbook, I visited the high school for a consulting session with the school's principal. Just as I entered the school, the principal saw me coming down the hallway and commented that he was excited to show me what the school had accomplished from his principal playbook. He shared that he and the English department chair had just left a social studies department meeting. They were working hard at leading their school in creating an efficient argumentative writing plan for the semester. The goals and action steps written in his principal playbook were actually happening, and he couldn't contain his excitement. The English department had tried several times to get an authentic, results-driven writing plan up and going, but it had never happened. Something always seemed to bog the writing initiative down, and their progress never seemed to last. But this year, the principal had written a goal that the English department and the social studies department would work together on an argumentative writing project where students would complete three pieces in that semester. This principal not only got that argumentative writing goal with the English and social studies departments off the ground but also actually accomplished all five of his principal playbook goals that semester. Things were moving forward. The school's vision was becoming a reality.

One reason the playbook is so critical is that it acts as a checklist to keep you on track and help you get things done. Thanks to the scholarly work of Atul Gawande (2009), surgeon and author of *The Checklist Manifesto*, it's plain that checklists can build confidence and lessen doubt of leaders (as cited in Shepard, 2020). Gawande (2009) created a simple checklist for operating room procedures called the Surgical Safety Checklist. Before a surgery begins, all people involved in the surgical procedure review the checklist, own responsibility for their part, and voice any concerns before the procedure begins. After putting the checklist in place, there was a 47 percent decrease in the death rate for surgeries performed where the surgical team used the checklist. And people who adopted checklists in fields beyond medicine, such as construction and aviation, also had these sorts of improvements (Gawande, 2009).

The principal playbook helped me create a checklist of critical work that our school needed to do, and it can help you do the same. Once you write the goals, work to put the specific, necessary steps in place to get the goals accomplished and running smoothly. A playbook can build a culture of teamwork where all people listed in the playbook's goals know their role, contribute their work, and are held accountable by the rest of the team.

Question 3: How Do You Develop a Principal Playbook?

The principal playbook covers one semester at a time. Usually, each of the four pages contains one or two goals. The number of goals on each page is a decision you and your leadership team make. The order of the pages is also entirely up to you and your team. Be careful not to take on too many goals. Prioritize the most critical work, and then set goals for the work that your school can achieve that semester. Some schools are able to complete two goals on each page, for a total of eight goals, that semester. Other schools need to focus on ELA and will have three to four goals on that page, with minimal goals on the other pages. Don't become discouraged by setting too many goals.

With the goals set, the principal thinks through action steps and places these in the principal playbook to ensure each step is clear. It is important to be specific with precisely *who* takes responsibility for *what* action to be completed by *when*. A *metric* verifies with evidence that the work has been accomplished. Complete all four columns of the principal playbook (figure 2.4, page 36) during the planning stage, including the specific metric that you will use. Once you have completed the goals, you can figure out the action steps and what evidence will be necessary. Because of the accountability measures in many schools in the subjects of English language arts and mathematics, many principals begin the goal setting with these subjects. Then they add the other subjects as quickly as possible so all teachers are involved in developing the best instructional practices.

Figures 2.5 (page 40) and 2.6 (page 41) show examples of playbook pages from schools where I have worked with principals on developing their principal playbooks. And figure 2.7 (page 42) shows an example of one I created myself during the course of my work in the New Albany Floyd County Consolidated School Corporation. You'll notice that one principal prefers to record the goal in bold and then give each action step its own row. Another prefers to record the bolded goal and then list the specific action steps directly following the goal. Principals should use the formatting that feels best for them.

Who	What	By When	Metric
All teachers, excluding mathematics	**Complete one argumentative writing piece each quarter.**	November 25 (first piece)	Five writing samples from each teacher per quarter
Barb (literacy coach)	Meet with English teachers to create professional development on the six essential components of an argumentative piece for all teachers. Mathematics teachers will be included in professional development to build their knowledge base. • Determine a graphic organizer to use. • Create a yes-or-no rubric for the six essentials. • Create a four-level rubric for the six essentials.	July 30	Professional development agenda Yes-or-no rubric Four-level rubric
English teachers	Facilitate the argumentative writing professional development for all teachers.	August 20	Teacher professional development feedback form
Barb	Conduct a follow-up meeting with all departments to determine possible topics for the first quarter's complex texts that match their units of study. • Social studies • Science • Art • Band, choir, and general music • Health and physical education • Project Lead the Way	Weeks of August 20 and 27	Department list of topics
Barb and department chairs	Locate two to three complex texts for each department to review, and then meet with each department chair.	September 15	List of selected complex texts by department
English teachers	Create partnerships with one English teacher to each department for review of the complex text, rubric, and modeling of Read, Discuss, Write strategy.	October 15	Notes from paired sessions
English department chair	Model the Read, Discuss, Write strategy in a full faculty meeting with additional modeling of the yes-or-no rubric.	October 30	Video of modeling
All teachers, excluding mathematics	Complete the first argumentative writing piece.	November 5–25	Five sample student writing pieces
Barb and English teachers	Lead Wednesday morning collaboration meetings where teachers bring student examples and rubric data to determine specific areas of need for follow-up instruction in English classes.	December 3 and 4	Areas of need list by grade level
All teachers, excluding mathematics	Complete the second argumentative writing piece.	December 19	Five sample student writing pieces

Source: © 2019 by Parkview Middle School. Used with permission.

Figure 2.5: Semester 1 principal playbook, ELA example.

Who	What	By When	Metric
Abbey (principal) and mathematics teachers Each mathematics teacher	**Review and revise our mathematics common formative assessments. Find areas of concern and more rigorous examples to incorporate. Work on this throughout quarter 1, and then make revisions. Do the same for quarter 2.** Quarter 1 • Keep notes of concerns and possible examples to incorporate. • Hold a CFA review meeting for quarter 1 to discuss notes and examples. • Make a consensus decision for revisions, and make those revisions. Quarter 2 • Keep notes of concerns and possible examples to incorporate. • Hold a CFA review meeting for quarter 2 to discuss notes and examples. • Make a consensus decision for revisions, and make those revisions. • Revised mathematics CFAs for the first semester are ready for next year!	 Throughout quarter 1 October 1 October 30 Throughout quarter 2 December 12 January 20 January 20	Quarters 1 and 2 CFAs revised
Maggie E. (mathematics teacher leader) with all mathematics teachers	**Establish a better and more specific dialogue around CFA quarterly data. Each quarter, select one learning target (at each grade level) where students did not achieve at 80 percent. Research to find a new instructional strategy, learn and practice the new strategy, reteach with that strategy, and reassess for next steps.** • Determine the learning target (for the first quarter, look at last year's data). • Spend collaboration time to research a new instructional strategy and have professional development. • Reteach the learning target with a new strategy. • Reassess. • Review new results. • List specifically both instructional strategies on the pacing guide with resources linked.	 August 3 August 5, 12, and 19 August 20–28 September 2–4 September 9 January 12	New strategy on the pacing guide for the specific learning target (area of concern)—one for each quarter

Figure 2.6: Semester 1 principal playbook, mathematics example.

Who	What	By When	Metric
Seventh-grade social studies teachers Literacy coach English teacher	Develop an engaging scenario for units 5 and 6. • Meet with all seventh-grade social studies teachers to review any current scenarios and brainstorm ideas for units 5 and 6 best options. • Select best engaging scenario options and use in one or two classes for a trial run. • Get student feedback from trial run and make necessary changes or revisions for units 5 and 6. • Develop rubric for the final version of each engaging scenario. • Add units 5 and 6 engaging scenario to pacing guide ready for second semester	December 15 August 30 September 30 October 15 November 5 December 1	Engaging scenario for units 5 and 6 on pacing guide and ready to go for second semester
Seventh-grade social studies teachers Literacy coach English teacher	Develop a writing activity for units 5 and 6. • Meet with all seventh-grade social studies teachers to brainstorm ideas for units 5 and 6 writing activity. Include literacy coach and one English teacher. • Finalize a selection for writing activities for units 5 and 6. • Develop rough draft of rubric for each writing activity (literacy coach and English teacher). • Meet with all seventh-grade social studies teachers for literacy coach and English teacher to review the writing activity rubrics. • Make any necessary revisions. • Add writing activities for units 5 and 6 to pacing guide ready for second semester.	December 15 September 15 September 30 October 15 October 30 November 5 November 30	Writing activity (with rubric) for units 5 and 6 developed and ready to be used for second semester

Figure 2.7: Semester 1 principal playbook, social studies example.

The work that the teachers did together in developing the engaging scenarios for their units, in creative and deliberate ways, was always a joy to watch. They were determined to find ways to engage their students in the learning for that unit. The engaging scenario for seventh-grade social studies unit 5, South Asia, looked something like this:

> You are the President of India and there have been many complaints that the former "Untouchables" are still living in severe poverty. Thoroughly investigate ways that your country could work to improve the standard of living for these citizens. Develop a plan, using industrialization and urbanization, to help these people. Write your State of the Union Address to solve the critical issue of poverty. In your State of the Union Address, present at least three specific possibilities, including industrialization and/or urbanization, to assist your people. A panel of distinguished guests will be in attendance to hear your address and provide feedback.

On the other systems page of the principal playbook, you simply determine the systems from your systems list that need to be addressed during that semester. Some systems will demand your attention immediately, and other systems will have to wait their turn to get a spot on the playbook. After a few semesters as principal, I realized I needed to address one system in particular because the situation was occurring each semester and we had no system in place. We needed a way to address teachers' requests that students be removed from the high-ability program. Teachers would come to my office and demand that a particular student be removed from a high-ability class because that student wasn't completing homework assignments. In previous years at the school, the teacher had simply needed to call the parents and inform them that their student was being removed. End of story. Easy out. I knew that was not the right thing to do. But we didn't have a system in place for handling that situation. At that time, we didn't have a district procedure in place either; it was left to the discretion of the individual school. Our school staff needed to have discussion around this topic, educate ourselves more about the makeup of a high-ability student, and establish a process for removing a student from the class or the entire program. This final page in the principal playbook gave me space to plan for this process. Figure 2.8 shows an example of another systems page from my own playbook.

Who	What	By When	Metric
Two high-ability teachers, two general education teachers, and Rhonda (principal)	Develop a system for requests to remove a student from a high-ability course or the entire program.	December 19	Completion of the system to remove students from high-ability courses or the program
Rhonda	Set up a meeting with all high-ability teachers and a district administrator for an informational session on high-ability students (qualification procedures, testing clarifications, high-ability models, and so on).	August 15	Notes from the session
Rhonda	Select a high-ability teacher leader to facilitate next steps.	August 30	Teacher on board
Megan (high-ability teacher leader)	Facilitate a meeting with all high-ability teachers to create a process for removal from a high-ability course or the program.	September 30	Draft of the system document
All high-ability teachers	Conduct a trial run of the newly developed process, debrief to make any necessary revisions, and finalize the plan.	October 30	Revisions completed on the draft
Megan	Meet with the district administrator to review the plan and gain permission to move forward.	November 15	Permission with the district administrator's signature
Megan and one high-ability teacher	Present and share the system in a faculty meeting with all staff members.	November 30	Faculty meeting notes
Teaching staff	The new system for removal from the high-ability program begins.	January 5	Copy of the system document in the faculty handbook

Figure 2.8: Semester 1 principal playbook, other systems example.

Here's what the finalized system for removal from a high-ability course looked like: when a teacher had concerns and would like a student removed from a high-ability course or the entire program, the teacher would take the following steps.

1. The teacher completes the request form for removal from the high-ability program, stating the reasons for removal, including relevant data.

2. The teacher contacts the parent to schedule a conference for discussion.

3. The counselor contacts the other participants in the conference.

4. The conference is held with the student, the parent, the high-ability teacher, two other teachers of the student, the counselor, and the administrator.

5. A thirty-day plan is established and put into place.

6. A conference is reconvened to review information and data from the thirty-day plan.

7. A conference decision determines the best placement for the student.

This system was actually one of the items we mentioned in our comprehensive inventory exercise that helped us create our systems list. It felt good to mark this one off our systems list and have a procedure in place.

The principal playbook was an invaluable tool to keep me focused on instruction and learning. That's why there are three pages (English language arts, mathematics, and other subjects) to set goals and action steps to keep learning as the priority. Effective principals always want to know what and how their students are learning in their schools. These pages will assist you in keeping your focus there. Then the final page of other systems helps to keep your school running smoothly and efficiently for everyone. When all of the systems are effective, you can spend so much more time on the continual strengthening of the academic core.

Question 4: When Do You Share the Principal Playbook?

As principal, I would prepare the principal playbook with the goals for the upcoming semester. Then I would discuss these goals with the leadership team in our summer off-site meeting. Team members would have a genuine and unfiltered conversation and determine if these were the most strategic items to include, if other things should be added, or if some things should be removed for a later semester. Then, the leadership team and I shared the revised principal playbook with our staff on the school's opening day in July.

Question 5: When Do You Update and Revise the Principal Playbook?

Once you have determined the goals for each page, you usually do not revise them during the semester. But you may have to tweak the action steps throughout the semester to allow for date changes and other minor adjustments. At the end of the semester, principals need to review the goals to see everything that's been accomplished. Ideally, every single goal will have been achieved.

You can remove the goals that have been completed and embedded in the school to make room in the playbook for the new semester goals. If the completed goals remain in the playbook, the document becomes lengthy and cumbersome. It's best to include only the current semester goals. Some principals create a comprehensive list of all accomplished goals, with the dates the work was completed (for example, a line item might read, "Mathematics CFAs revised—fall 2020"). It can be rewarding to review the comprehensive list each semester with the leadership team and your entire staff to see how much progress your school is making.

Some principals have concerns with putting only a few goals in each semester's playbook. They may lack clarity as to what to do with all the other things needing to be done for their school. Not everything can go in the playbook—only the most critical items that need focus and immediate attention for that particular semester. Choose the most important academic work that the school needs to address for the ELA, mathematics, and other subjects pages; choose the most important systems that the school needs to address for the other systems page. In the meanwhile, do the necessary work for items not in the playbook. Keep those things running as smoothly as possible, knowing that they all will become priorities soon and receive the attention they need. Robert Eaker and Douglas Reeves (2020) suggest that "when leaders try to do too many things—even with the best of intentions—little gets done" (p. 13).

Get the Big Rocks in Place First

The principal playbook is an effective tool for you to use in prioritizing the work. You, along with the leadership team, carefully select the goals to accomplish for the semester. Kim Marshall (2008), a principal in Boston Public Schools for thirty-two years, uses an analogy of filling a jar with rocks and pebbles. First, you must identify the big rocks of the needed work, the ones with the highest priority. Always remember the big rocks are the ones "that drive high achievement" (Marshall, 2008, p. 17). If you do not wisely select those priorities and then strategically schedule them within your daily schedule, they won't get done. All the little pebbles—the numerous requests from staff, the running from one fire to the next, the unimportant meetings—will take almost all your time and prevent you from intentionally focusing on the work required to accomplish the big rocks. If you don't place the big rocks in the jar first, you'll never get them in because the little pebbles will take up all the space. Get the big rocks—the most critical goals—in your principal playbook, and get going!

To reflect on clarifying the essential work and begin work on your next steps, see the reproducible tools on pages 46–49.

Systems Review Checklist

If you haven't organized your systems (after doing the comprehensive inventory exercise) or you simply need to review your list, the following rubric is an easy-to-use tool that can help you gain a clear understanding of which systems are solid, which need minor changes, which need major work, and which are systems in name only—that is, you've named the system but have not begun work on it. If a system listed here is not applicable to your school, simply cross it out. Add other necessary systems in the spaces provided at the end of the checklist. Look back to the systems list example on page 34 for more details.

System	System Solid and Embedded	Minor Changes or Additions Necessary	Major Work Necessary	System in Name Only
Academic core				
Anti-racism initiatives				
Assembly procedures				
Assessments				
Athletics and extracurriculars				
Cafeteria procedures				
Classroom management				
Closing day awards program				
Closing-of-school procedures				
Communication system				
Community outreach and engagement				
Data collection process and data-driven conversations				
Dual language program				
English learner placement and program				
Facilities				
Finances and budget				
High-ability placement process and requests for removal from program				
Highly effective teacher process for opportunities to strengthen the school				
Induction of new students to the building *during the year*				
Interviewing, hiring, and induction program for new teachers				
Noncertified personnel system for success				
Opening days with teachers				
Opening-of-school procedures				

page 1 of 2

System	System Solid and Embedded	Minor Changes or Additions Necessary	Major Work Necessary	System in Name Only
Parent-teacher night (open house)				
Parent-teacher organization				
Parent-teacher or student-led conferencing				
PreK system and day care relationships				
Schedules (all)				
School safety and security				
Schoolwide behavior model				
Six meetings of leadership (see chapter 5, page 83)				
Social-emotional system for staff well-being				
Social-emotional system for student well-being				
Social media expectations of staff				
Special education procedures (including Section 504)				
Staff personal- and sick-day procedures				
Strategic scheduling for students and staff				
Student transfer requests				
Substitute teachers				
Teacher improvement plan process				
Teacher observations and evaluation conversations				
Technology initiatives and virtual learning				
Transitions *from* elementary school and transitions *to* high school				

Systems Next Steps Chart

Once you've completed the "Systems Review Checklist" (page 46), choose two systems that need immediate focus. If you have more than two systems you want to include on the semester's principal playbook, just make another copy of this sheet for as many systems as you need. Write these systems in the following template, begin to research as many ideas as possible to build and strengthen these systems, talk with fellow administrators about their current practices, and jot down the next steps necessary for developing your own systems. Once you have a final plan in place, place these two systems (or more) in your principal playbook for the current or next semester's work.

System 1	System 2
List of ideas and actions necessary to build or strengthen this system:	List of ideas and actions necessary to build or strengthen this system:
Next Steps	Next Steps

Principal Playbook Semester Goals

Now that you've developed or revised your systems list and selected goals for your principal playbook, use the following template to list the basic goals on each page of your principal playbook. You can begin with one or two goals per page. Remember, some principals do not use the other subjects page until they feel the ELA, mathematics, and other systems pages are solidified and working well. The purpose of this activity is to help you prioritize the goals for the semester and get them listed in your principal playbook. You can go back later to develop the action steps for each goal.

Semester 1 Principal Playbook, ELA and Literacy

Who	What	By When	Metric

Semester 1 Principal Playbook, Mathematics

Who	What	By When	Metric

Semester 1 Principal Playbook, Other Subjects

Who	What	By When	Metric

Semester 1 Principal Playbook, Other Systems (Use the two systems from the "Systems Next Steps Chart," page 48.)

Who	What	By When	Metric

CHAPTER 3

Create Teams to Move the Work Forward

You have established a vision of what your school can look like in two to three years. You have a principal playbook with the semester's prioritized goals and clarified work. Now you need help to accomplish this work! That's where your school's teams come into play.

Grade-level teams and department teams, made up of teachers responsible for the same content at that grade level or subject area, are essential in moving the work forward. These teacher teams will accomplish the goals in the principal playbook. In this chapter, however, we will focus on the essential leadership action of creating two other teams that support and guide the grade-level and department teams: (1) the leadership team and (2) the teacher leader team. We'll start with your school's leadership team. We will discuss the key foundations and introduce three key understandings of leadership teams: (1) the leadership team's purpose and member responsibilities, (2) the right members for the leadership team, and (3) the right number of people for the leadership team. Then we will look at the significance of your teacher leader team, whose members are usually part of the leadership team, and the development of its role. We'll consider ways to select teachers wisely, provide training, check in regularly, and create the professional development calendar with them.

Know the Key Foundations of the Leadership Team

Principals need to have a clear understanding of what it means to be a team. My experience has taught me that teams involve people who have come together around a shared vision and common goals. Teams are aligned with that vision and those goals. Effective team members work interdependently and truly depend on one another. They demonstrate a collective commitment to the work and are accountable to each other. When staff members aren't functioning this way, you probably just have a group of people *meeting* together, not a team of people *working* together. Effective principals want to build teams that will outlast them. They want to create teams where members serve one another, make sacrifices together, and continually commit to the work of making their school better.

Stop for a minute to consider all the sports and academic teams you have in your school. Then consider whether your current leadership team works more like a golf team or a basketball team. A golf team typically has six members; all members each try to play their own best match and then bring back their individual score at the conclusion of the round. All the individual golfers' scores are combined for a final product. A basketball team has five members on the court at one time, who play together, work together, and achieve the final score as a group. It's a simple analogy. Do the members of your leadership team work more like a golf team or a basketball team? Do they only care about their individual work, their particular grade level or department? Teachers working in a group never actually become a team, as DuFour and colleagues (2016) explain:

> until members must rely on one another to accomplish a goal that none could achieve individually . . . [and] engage in a systematic process in which they work together, interdependently, to analyze and impact their professional practice in order to improve individual and collective results. (p. 60)

Early in my tenure as principal, I knew that our leadership team members were acting as individuals doing their own thing, representing their own interests, and not working together toward a specific target. It was very clear to me that we needed to become much more interdependent. We needed to be a team that valued collective responsibility to maximally align the work of the school.

As I reflected on the way the leadership team was interacting, I remembered an experience from my early years of teaching. I served on the school's leadership team and represented the English department. If I'm honest, I truly only cared about the needs and concerns of the English department and getting those issues on the agenda as discussable items. We needed more time for instruction and more resources. I didn't have a true concern for the mathematics teachers or other departments. I concentrated my focus on my particular needs, not the needs or health of the organization as a whole.

Our principal, as building leader, didn't help me and my fellow leadership team members comprehend that key understanding of working together as a team. Instead, he established a culture where we each needed to be ready with our data and solid arguments in order to get what we wanted. No real listening took place in our time together. We just prepared our presentations and waited for our turn to convince the other members to do what we wanted. As I think back on those early years of my teaching, I wish I'd known what I understand now. That leadership team should have pulled together to use our individual strengths as department leaders to help elevate the overall team and school performance. We had to unite for our school if we were serious about achieving higher results. But we didn't. We only cared about our own particular group.

As a principal, you must not underestimate the importance of your leadership team. Your team needs to pull together, putting aside individual preferences and placing the needs of the group above all. Simon Sinek (2017), author and motivational speaker, agrees with this necessity when he writes that "the ability of a group of people to do remarkable things hinges on how well those people can pull together as a team" (p. 139).

Consider Three Key Understandings for the Leadership Team

Let's move into the principal's work of creating the leadership team while keeping these three understandings about the leadership team in mind: (1) its purpose and member responsibilities, (2) the right members for the team, and (3) the right number of people for the team.

Understanding 1: The Leadership Team's Purpose and Member Responsibilities

The leadership team is the direct link between you and all your staff members. This team mainly comprises staff members who represent a particular department or grade level. The team is led by you as the principal and often meets biweekly. The number of meetings may vary for some schools. Many schools' leadership teams meet biweekly for a couple of meetings in the beginning of the year to make certain clear expectations are set and then shift to meeting monthly. The main responsibilities of the leadership team members include the following.

- Discuss in detail the goals of the principal playbook and progress toward those goals.

- Clarify the required work of the department or grade level with all teachers they represent, and offer support when needed.

- Make certain the department or grade level understands it is required to do the work, not invited to do the work or given an option to do the work.

- Dig deep into the student learning data of the department or grade level to prioritize instructional changes and revisions.

- Share teacher instructional examples and student work samples with the rest of the team.

- Work with the teacher leaders to find support and resources for the department or grade level.

- Listen to how the work is progressing in other departments or grade levels to gain any helpful information to use in members' own areas.

- Discuss any department or grade-level struggles, and assist in brainstorming and implementing solutions.

- Ensure that the necessary changes within the department or grade level are actually taking place and are embedded in classroom instruction.

- Communicate in a clear, effective, and timely manner with each person that members represent.

Understanding 2: The Right Members for the Leadership Team

The next key understanding for consideration is selecting the members of your leadership team. Many principals inherit a leadership team when they become principal of their school. When these principals begin working with that team, it's important that they immediately share the team's purpose and clarify members' responsibilities. A few members may choose to remove themselves from the team once they have a clear understanding of the work ahead. One or more of the team members may be a Fundamentalist, which consultant and author Anthony Muhammad (2018) describes as an "experienced educator who believes that there is one pure and undisputable way to practice: the traditional model of schooling" (p. 77). But don't give up on the Fundamentalists too quickly. When you lead the work with solid reasoning and meaningful data, even the Fundamentalists can become essential members of the team: "Rationale means everything. When they understand, they cooperate" (Muhammad, 2018, p. 124).

When you have open spots to fill, carefully consider staff members who could possibly serve on the leadership team. It's important to think about how the rest of the school perceives the potential members. Are they viewed as teachers and staff members who demonstrate the essentials of the school's core purpose? Do they believe students can achieve at high levels? Do they believe their instruction and work are the key factors for their students' achievement?

Think about adjectives and phrases you would want your staff to use to describe the members of your leadership team. You might have the current members of your leadership team engage in the exercise of thinking about the qualities and characteristics of an ideal team member. Have them think about it for several minutes and then write down, on their own paper, a few adjectives or phrases they would use to describe the ideal team member for their school. Next, have team members share out the adjectives and phrases on their notes, with one person capturing all of them and writing them on the whiteboard or chart paper so all team members can see them clearly. Words and phrases like *kind, honest, really works hard, has great relationships with everyone, transparent, sees the big picture*, and *dedicated* often appear. Take your time as you lead this exercise and get all the positive aspects listed.

For the closing of this exercise, place two categories on the board: (1) Current and (2) Aspiring. Explain to the team members that they have listed adjectives and phrases of ideal team members. Now they are to decide whether the majority of the team exhibits these qualities. Encourage your team members to be honest. Take one adjective or phrase at a time. Are they currently, as a team, seen as *kind*? If so, place it under the Current category. If not, place it under the Aspiring category. The goal of the exercise is to select two to three words or phrases that the leadership team currently embodies and two to three words or phrases that the team aspires to become. You could keep these positive reminders posted in your office and then use them in conversations as your team strives to work together in the aspirational ways.

You may find that one or more of your current team members are not capable of demonstrating the positive attributes that the team has selected. Effective principals have honest dialogue with these individual members and discuss in detail the specific concerns and what needs to occur in the future. After a few months of working together, or even a semester, if the member is still not making the required changes, then you must remove the team member. The right people need to be serving on the team. Author Jim Collins (2001), who does research on company sustainability and growth, compares leaders to bus drivers and writes we leaders must first get "the right people on the bus, the wrong people off the bus, and the right people in the right seats—and then" we'll figure out "where to drive it" (p. 13).

The critical factor for principals is to select teachers who are both competent and caring. This factor is echoed in the remarks of Steve Gruenert (2019), professor and author on school culture, who states that leadership team members must be "highly effective with high positive influence. In other words, these people must be respected and connected." It falls to the principal to figure out who these influencers are and get them on the team. Gruenert and Todd Whitaker (2015), in cowriting the book *School Culture Rewired* with exercises to help identify influencers and displaying their passion for school culture and leadership, write:

> It's important to understand that influencers are always influencing—theirs isn't a hobby, it's a lifestyle. Influencers live for opportunities to share stories with others. Some share stories that align with your plans for moving the culture forward; others tell stories in service of maintaining the status quo. It's up to you to determine which group wins. (p. 160)

By using the rating matrices in Gruenert and Whitaker's (2015) book that help you plot and graph the relationships you're aware of among your school's teachers, you can help determine the best members for your leadership team.

Understanding 3: The Right Number of People for the Leadership Team

Finally, principals must understand that they have to give serious consideration to the number of people on the leadership team. Lencioni (2012) suggests that "so many teams . . . struggle simply because they're too large. This is a big problem and a common one. A leadership team should be made up of somewhere between three and twelve people" (p. 21). Why is this consideration critical? Because as a leader, you are trying to maintain balance between advocacy and inquiry. If too many people are on the team, members begin to advocate for their department or grade-level wants or needs. Explanations and arguments of why one particular need is more important than another need not consume too much meeting time. Once again, the focus moves from the health of the whole school to the health of one department or grade level, from making decisions based on what's best for the entire building to making decisions based on the loudest or most demanding team member. Instead of allowing team members to just advocate for their own needs, the principal must skillfully model a spirit of inquiry about each other's needs. Principals can ask inquiry questions like, "Why do you feel that's most important for our school? Do you understand the real needs in each of our departments? Can you help me understand a little more about your comments? From all the information we have, how would you prioritize the needs in our school?" Principals must model inquiry instead of advocacy.

By modeling inquiry, you try to ensure that leadership team members aren't coming to meetings to lobby. Again, this is why the number of people on the team is important—so members feel assured that they will have time to express their thoughts, have meaningful discussion, and ask questions of others on the team. You can't allow one group to turn against another group. Your leadership must make it clear that your decisions are about the health of the entire school. And it must guide your team members to listen to one another, to work hard at truly understanding one another, and to make decisions in the school's best interests. Once your team is working in this manner, real change begins to take hold, and the positive effects begin to multiply.

Figure 3.1 shows the makeup of the leadership team in our middle school with grades 5–8, which had approximately nine hundred students. The teachers who served as members of the leadership team represented their content-area teams, and we also had two teachers who represented both fifth and sixth grades and seventh and eighth grades.

Figure 3.2 shows how a leadership team might look in a smaller elementary and secondary school.

Your leadership team should also include your school's full-time instructional coaches, if you're lucky enough to have any. It's key that every staff member in your school have a representative on the leadership team. All staff members must have a link to a leadership team member in order to gain the information, clarity, and support they need.

Position
Principal
Assistant principal
Grade-level counselor
English teacher
Mathematics teacher
Social studies teacher
Science teacher
Elective teacher
Special education teacher
Fifth- and sixth-grade teacher
Seventh- and eighth-grade teacher
Literacy coach

Figure 3.1: Middle school leadership team makeup.

Elementary School	Secondary School
Principal	Principal
Grades K–2 teacher	Counselor
Grades 3–5 teacher	English teacher
Elective teacher	Mathematics teacher
Special education teacher	Elective teacher
	Special education teacher

Figure 3.2: Leadership team makeup at a smaller elementary and secondary school.

Build the Teacher Leader Team

Now that I've discussed three key understandings of the leadership team, there is one other team to discuss: the teacher leader team, which comprises teachers who step up to lead and support their fellow teachers. These teacher leaders assist in leading the department or grade-level meetings, supporting fellow teachers, and providing professional development. These same teacher leaders serve on the leadership team, but there will be times throughout the semester when you, as principal, will meet specifically with the teacher leaders to guide the instructional focus. These teachers are invaluable to you as principal. They are the critical pieces in the school's ability to move forward and make progress instructionally.

Some schools are fortunate and have enough resources to have a full-time instructional coach or two on staff who can fulfill this role. You may have a literacy coach, a mathematics coach, or an instructional coach who coordinates both subjects. These coaches' critical responsibility is to support teachers in their instruction and to genuinely help teachers grow. They understand that there must be quality initial instruction in every classroom. They assist teachers in using strategies correctly and consistently over time. They develop and nurture positive relationships, get resources when needed, model and demonstrate continued learning, and network with as many teachers as they can. If you have full-time instructional coaches at your school, again I recommend they be part of your leadership team. Some schools have one instructional coach and then use teacher leaders for the other subject areas. For example, our middle school had a full-time literacy coach. She worked with our English and special education teachers for the most part. Then teacher leaders were selected for the other subject areas.

Let's consider four things about your school's teacher leaders: (1) select wisely, (2) provide training, (3) check in regularly, and (4) create a professional development calendar.

Select Wisely

Whether you have instructional coaches, teacher leaders, or a combination of both, you should make it a priority to carefully select and develop these staff members. They will assist you in driving the school forward and reaching your vision.

Select teachers who are capable of working collaboratively with all members of the grade level or department they will be working with. It is imperative that these teachers have the ability to build trust so that real coaching can take place. Effective principals know the most difficult work happens in the classrooms as teachers address the individual learning needs of each of their students. Because of this work's intensity and teachers' need for support, principals select teacher leaders who can truly help. Many teachers are not comfortable having someone else in their classroom. Some worry that a teacher leader is nothing more than a spy for their principal to gain information to use against them for evaluative purposes. You must make certain to get the right people in these teacher leader positions.

Teacher leaders must be able to establish expectations for their classroom observations, coaching and modeling visits, data review meetings, and the clear teacher goals they set for the next few weeks. They are clear on the specific actions that will take place in weekly department and grade-level meetings. They also assist in setting clear expectations for the collaboration meetings that many schools hold weekly before or after school where grade-level and department teams continue their work together. And through each and every one of these responsibilities, these teacher leaders must listen to their colleagues and diligently work to establish rapport for continued growth.

When selecting these teacher leaders, think about teachers who are capable of giving and receiving critical feedback. These teachers clearly communicate the school's goals and initiatives. And they also clearly communicate the areas of expertise within the grade-level or department teams. Teacher leaders spend time studying with their department and grade-level colleagues, trying action research projects, and improving student learning.

Ideal teacher leaders genuinely care about their students. They know their content and can deliver it well. They create dynamic lessons and have the ability to help others do the same. They're accessible to teachers on their teams, and they have a sense of urgency in putting in place the playbook goals identified for their department or grade level.

If teachers in the school don't have respect for their teacher leaders, the grade level or department will accomplish almost nothing. It's a horrible situation to have a teacher leader in place without any real change occurring. If that happens, you must make the tough decision of finding another teacher with the right qualities for the leadership position. Some teachers are phenomenal in the classroom with students, but this does not always translate to being a phenomenal teacher leader.

When possible, some principals build their master schedule to make it so the teacher leaders can teach two or three periods each day. Then the teacher leaders spend the remainder of the day on coaching responsibilities and planning. Sometimes, a teacher leader can coach and assist only one period each day. And often, the teacher leader's schedule doesn't have any time for coaching and supporting, so principals cover classrooms and hire substitutes to provide the necessary time for the teacher leader to work with other teachers.

Provide Training

Once you have chosen teachers with highly effective instructional skills and the greatest positive influence with other staff members, they'll require appropriate training. Of course, you will provide professional development for curricular needs. But don't leave out some basic coaching on listening, building trust, handling conflict, and facilitating difficult conversations. These are non-negotiables for teacher leader training. Provide these teachers with professional learning opportunities, consistent time to collaborate, and time to engage in reflective practices as they lead the curricular work of the school.

I learned about teacher leader training the hard way. When I served as a director of middle schools for the New Albany Floyd County schools, our three middle school principals and I were so excited to have created a full-time position for a district middle school English language arts coach. The teacher chosen for this position, Leslie—who was previously a sixth-grade ELA teacher at one of the middle schools—would work with all three middle schools' ELA teachers on a rotating basis. We developed a three-week cycle where she could spend an entire week at a time in one school, visiting every ELA classroom, assisting teachers, modeling lessons, and securing needed resources. Leslie had implemented the district's literacy framework within her own classroom, helped a few other teachers in her own middle school, and achieved consistent results with her students before earning the district position.

After the interviewing process with all three of the middle school principals, Leslie was selected. At our first middle school administrative team meeting with all principals and counselors, I introduced Leslie to the entire group, reviewed her visitation schedule, and welcomed her on board. Then I sent her off to go meet twenty-five new ELA teachers in buildings where she'd never worked, and I assumed things would go as well as they had in her home school. It didn't quite work out that way. About four weeks into the school year, Leslie dropped by my office and collapsed in the chair in front of my desk.

"This is really hard work!" she said. "Teachers are getting defensive with me, asking me so many questions, and some of them don't even want me coming in their rooms. They think I'm just there to report back to you and the principals. I need some help, or I might just need to go back to my own classroom. I didn't think it would be this hard." And then Leslie let out a long sigh and looked to me for guidance.

I felt horrible. We had a solid induction program for new middle school teachers, but I had thrown Leslie right out there with no induction at all. I knew she was successful in her own classroom and in her own school, so I had assumed the other schools and teachers would naturally trust her and allow her to assist them. I was wrong. Learn from my mistake. Provide coaching books and materials and, if at all possible, some in-person professional development to prepare teacher leaders for the position. Provide an induction program and mentor teacher leaders throughout their first year.

Check In Regularly

Principals need to regularly collaborate with their teacher leaders to develop a clear vision of next steps for each subject area or grade level. This includes the goals in the principal playbook and specific areas of work for particular teachers. Your teacher leaders are involved in decision making and are responsible for keeping each member of the grade level or department strategically involved in the current work. Tune in to your teacher leaders' thoughts, listen to their ideas and advice, and always be open to their recommendations.

These systematic debriefings or check-ins are critical to knowing what the teacher leaders are seeing and knowing what support they need. One principal, in leading his biweekly school-improvement team meeting, asked teacher leaders to review the most recent data and current strategies. The discussion always included any resources that teachers needed.

Another teacher leader shared with me that she met with her principal every other week. They reviewed her department's focus on the specific area of learning from the principal playbook. She shared data, analyzed them deeply, and discussed possible next steps. She said her principal expected her to have a clear understanding of what was going on in other subjects too. Her principal expected her to report back to the teachers she represented to make certain they were aware of any vital information. She felt empowered as a teacher leader; she felt trusted to share information and next steps. She knew her principal trusted her, but she also knew he would verify things. She shared that her principal always followed up with the other teachers in her department. If she was not leading her grade level or department well, he would have a conversation with her. If things continued not going well, he'd get someone else. He made it clear to all the teacher leaders that he didn't have time to waste on inefficiency and he needed people who were going to communicate clearly and get teachers the support they needed. These regular check-ins with the teacher leaders are essential for you, the principal, to have the up-to-date information required to lead the school.

Create a Professional Development Calendar

Teacher leaders play a strategic role in developing a professional development calendar for the semester. This professional development should include full-day sessions where students are not in attendance and half-day sessions where particular grade levels and departments have substitutes in their classrooms so the teachers can attend the scheduled professional development. The most important professional development takes place *weekly* in one-hour sessions where grade-level teachers meet with the teacher leader to discuss data and develop instructional strategies to address deficiencies in student learning.

A semester professional development calendar captures all these sessions and lists the specific work each teacher group will be doing over the next two to three meetings. For example, let's consider a school where the grade-level or department teachers have planning time together once a week during the day for forty-five minutes. Their district has also built-in time for these same teachers to meet together for sixty minutes after school each week on Wednesday. The teacher leaders work with their grade-level or department team to determine and plan expectations and exactly what they will accomplish in those meetings. If the English department team members know they need to discuss and create a rubric for an argumentative writing piece, they may allow three or four meetings for this work. The seventh-grade mathematics teachers may be trying to find another teaching strategy to help their students understand slope. The teacher leaders organize the work they will do during the meeting times and report that to the principal. In this way, the principal is well informed about what all grade-level or department teams are working on during their meetings together.

Once teachers complete the meetings listed on the calendar, the principal can come for a follow-up visit with them to ask for products of their work. To follow up on the previous examples, the principal could ask for the argumentative writing rubric or the strategy selected to teach slope. Effective principals have no doubts or concerns about what teachers are doing during their grade-level or department meetings. They don't require agendas or notes following the meetings. Instead, they do the orchestrated and demanding work of following up with each grade-level or department team to witness the actual instructional changes that address the specific areas where students are struggling. These principals are strong administrators empowering teachers to lead their departments and grade levels. They lead with both an urgency to make things better and the patience to settle in for the long haul while the work gets done.

Enact Change Through Effective Teams

In summary, effective principals understand that their school teams are an integral and meaningful part of the school. John Hattie (2018), authority on education effectiveness from the University of Melbourne, Australia, says that teacher collective efficacy is the number one indicator of student learning. It's all about teachers working together in teams. It's more than teachers simply believing that they can make a difference; it's that they actually do make a difference! They meet together and work hard. They have high expectations for all students. They set goals for a year's growth and then find ways to make that growth occur. As Hattie (2018) puts it, "When you fundamentally believe you can make a difference and you feed it with the evidence that you are, then that is dramatically powerful." As principal of your school, you can't possibly do all the work alone. But with carefully created teams working together, you'll be able to drive the changes your school needs and see the results in students' learning growth.

To reflect on creating teams to move the work forward and begin work on your next steps, see the reproducible tools on pages 61–64.

Key Foundations of the Leadership Team

Reflect on the key foundations of a team.

- Shared vision
- Common goals
- Alignment with the vision and goals
- Collective commitment to the work
- Collaboration

Use the following template to jot down your own answers to the provided questions. Then, with your leadership team, facilitate discussion and come to consensus on any necessary changes for questions that you gave a *no* response.

Question	Yes or No	If No, What Needs to Change to Make This a Yes?
Does every member of our leadership team believe in the shared vision that we are working toward in the next two to three years, and can each of them articulate our shared vision?		
Do all members of our leadership team clearly understand the principal playbook goals for the current semester and their responsibility in achieving these goals?		
Does each member of our leadership team work to align the work of the school so that we are working in the same direction and developing cohesive learning for our students?		
Does each member of our leadership team commit to the work ahead and hold the other members accountable to that work?		
Does each member of our leadership team work interdependently and depend on the other members?		

Activities for Building the Leadership Team

Take time to do the following three activities as you build the strongest leadership team possible for your school.

Activity 1: Leadership Team Responsibilities Chart

Review the responsibilities of leadership team members, and then use the following chart to write specific names of team members needing support from you in those specific responsibilities. Schedule a time to discuss your concerns with these team members.

Leadership Team Responsibility	Team Members Who Need Support in This Responsibility
To discuss in detail the goals of the principal playbook and progress being made	
To clarify the required work of their department or grade level with all teachers they represent and offer support when needed	
To make certain their department or grade level understands it is required to do the work, not invited to do the work	
To dig deep into the student learning data of the department or grade level to prioritize instructional changes and revisions	
To share teacher instructional examples and student work samples from their department or grade level with the leadership team	
To listen to how the work is progressing in other departments or grade levels to gain any helpful information to use in their own area	
To discuss any department or grade-level struggles and to assist in brainstorming and implementing solutions with the leadership team	
To ensure the needed changes within the department or grade level are actually taking place and are embedded in the classroom instruction	
To communicate in a clear, effective, and timely manner with each person they represent	

The Deliberate and Courageous Principal © 2022 Solution Tree Press • SolutionTree.com
Visit **go.SolutionTree.com/leadership** to download this free reproducible.

Activity 2: Current and Aspiring Descriptors Chart

Complete this chart on your own to prepare your thoughts before doing the activity with the leadership team. Consider the most positive traits and characteristics of teachers serving on the current leadership team or any leadership teams from your past. Write them in the first column. Then take each of the positive descriptors and determine whether your leadership team as a whole currently demonstrates that descriptor or it aspires to do so. Place each positive descriptor in the second or third column as appropriate.

Positive Leadership Descriptors	Current Positive Leadership Descriptors	Aspiring Positive Leadership Descriptors

Activity 3: Leadership Team Chart

Now that you've thought through the leadership team's responsibilities and created your current and aspiring positive descriptors, complete the following chart with the positions and names of staff members you feel best match your positive descriptors to serve on the leadership team. Make certain every staff member in your building is represented by someone on the team, including yourself.

School Leadership Team Positions	Staff Names

The Deliberate and Courageous Principal © 2022 Solution Tree Press • SolutionTree.com
Visit **go.SolutionTree.com/leadership** to download this free reproducible.

Teacher Leader Team Rating Template

Rate your proficiency in each component of creating teacher leader teams using a scale of 1 to 5, 1 being the lowest level of proficiency and 5 being the highest. Then create a list of action steps you can take to strengthen your teacher leader team.

Rating (1–5)	Crucial Component of Building a Teacher Leader Team
	I carefully select teacher leaders who are highly effective and have the greatest positive influence to guide and support our faculty and staff in research-based best practices.
	I provide training for the teacher leaders and set clear expectations to continuously foster a culture where we strive to increase learning for all students.
	I facilitate meaningful dialogue in regular check-ins with each teacher leader.
	I make certain that each teacher leader works with me to create a professional development calendar for the semester to meet the needs of teachers and their instruction.
Principal Action Steps for Strengthening the Teacher Leader Team:	

CHAPTER 4

Take Action Instead of Being Busy

Y ou've established a vision, clarified the essential work using your principal playbook, developed your systems list, and created strategic teams to assist you. It's very clear that principals have an inordinate amount of work to do, and it's easy to get lost in the busyness of each day. Many principals begin each day with great intentions of accomplishing specific goals, but at day's end feel disappointed that they completed only one—or none—of those goals, despite the fact that their day was absolutely full. Being in constant motion can feel like progress. But don't be fooled. It's not. Taking action, not just being busy, is where principals make real progress.

James Clear (n.d.a), an author who focuses on the topic of how we can live better lives, describes this dilemma as the tension between taking action and being in motion; many principals may struggle to distinguish between the two and find it hard to organize their varied responsibilities. *Being in motion* involves getting pulled from one task to the next, reactively putting out each fire as it arises, and lacking certainty of which project needs full attention at the moment. This rushing from one thing to the next, whatever calls out the loudest, can lead principals into a stress-filled cycle that takes time away from the essential work of leading the team and staff toward the vision.

Principals encounter many potential distractions: talking with parents who stop by the building, monitoring the cafeteria each lunch period, supervising the dress code, dealing with technology issues, checking on sports facilities, processing behavior referrals, monitoring restrooms each break, picking up garbage around the school, completing state or provincial reports, returning phone calls, and supervising the car rider line. The list goes on and on. These are all important things. But focusing on these tasks will not create meaningful change for student learning. Other staff members can assist in many of these tasks. Effective principals don't become martyrs, thinking they have to do everything. They fully understand that being busy does not equate to high levels of student learning in classrooms.

Taking action is much more difficult. Effective principals focus their time on the most essential work: the principal playbook goals and action steps created with their leadership team. They prioritize their time on a daily basis to make certain the essential work is taking place each day. They make the time for what matters most for the advancement of classroom instruction. These effective principals are certainly busy, but they busy themselves with real action steps that create the conditions for everyone to be successful in their school.

In this chapter, I will look at three key areas to aid you in taking action instead of being busy to fight against the wave of nonessential activities. First, you must focus on building your systems. Second, you must manage time—every minute of it—efficiently. And last, you could create a helpful tool called the principal monthly guide. Let's get started.

Build Your Systems

I introduced systems in chapter 2 (page 29) as a page in the principal playbook; now it's time to go into further detail. Along with your leadership team, you created your own list of the multiple systems that are necessary to run an efficient and organized school. You may need to create some systems and revise others.

So often, I see principals working extremely hard. But many of them are working on the same things, year after year. Putting effective systems in place can help them prevent this. *Systems* are explicit, detailed procedures and information to help the varied components of the school run efficiently. These systems allow principals to create a solid, effective way of doing specific things. Effective principals essentially ask, "How can things get better here?" when creating systems. Every year, the principal can retrieve and renew a system, and it's ready to go. You'll find that after using systems, you can make tweaks and revisions to strengthen each of them even more. Prioritize the systems that need focus, place them on the other systems page of your principal playbook, and get to work.

School buildings feature many systems—large systems and smaller ones. It's not too difficult to develop structures for the smaller ones, but it's vital to have these systems running well. Smaller systems include things like the opening day with teachers, the substitute teacher system, or the closing-of-school procedure. Some of the larger systems can be complex, and it takes focused, intentional time to develop a detailed plan so they work for everyone involved. A few of these larger systems would include the academic core, teacher leader development, the new teacher induction program, anti-racism initiatives, and teacher improvement plans. It probably sounds like common sense to have these systems built and in place. But my experience has shown me that it's not common practice. You must make it a priority to get these fundamental systems documented, in place, and running efficiently.

In effective and high-performing schools, systems are in place to deal with the issues that arise on a day-to-day basis. Schools that have robust systems in place can handle these issues as they happen, while in other schools, these things could easily turn into emergencies. When emergencies don't consistently happen, administrators don't have to expend constant and immediate attention on such issues.

When systems are in place within the school, staff members know what to do and have clear processes to handle most situations. That doesn't mean you're not involved if they need help, but they don't have to consult you on every instance. Once again, you are not unresponsive. You respond if needed. But staff members are competent and capable of handling most situations with the developed system in place, so you can concentrate on classroom observations and meetings with staff.

There are two types of occurrences. The first is a situation that happens over and over again. The other type of occurrence is a one-time event. You, as principal, are often needed to help problem solve for this second type. For recurring situations, build systems. For example, every year you know you will need to have your substitute teacher system and your school safety system in place. These systems, once built, will serve you year after year and enable you and your leadership team to be proactive instead of reactive in the work of your school. When a one-time or unordinary event occurs, like an intruder in the school building, you will need to be right in the middle of handling such a situation. While you still have a system in place to help, this is a system you hope you never have to use. It's OK to hope these situations don't arise, but the unpredictability inherent in them means you'll be needed if they do.

Let me share one last thing about systems. Make certain you, as principal, know where you fit within the school's systems, not where you feel comfortable or particularly enjoy the work. Know where your leadership and authority are needed. One good example comes to mind. I was a school guidance counselor for many years. I really enjoyed those years because I was able to give support to students, teachers, and families. When I became a principal, I could easily get into lengthy conversations with parents who came to me with a concern that their child was being bullied. Sometimes, I would sit with a parent and discuss several options, develop a plan, and then call the guidance counselor to join us for a final review. That work took a lot of my time, and it was not in our school's best interest for me to be doing it. The school had a strong counseling team in place and had developed a system for bullying. I needed to use the system that had been developed and call upon our counselor to run that system. The counselors were more than capable and ready to put the details of the bullying system in place. And they did!

Let me be very honest here. Meeting with students and parents about bullying felt good to me. I felt like a hero. I was helping to solve their concerns, and they were extremely grateful. That work felt comfortable to me, and I felt competent doing it. But it was not my work to do. It took my attention off the essential work of the principal playbook. It undermined the school's competent and effective counselors. That was their work. Our counselors had developed an effective system, with lots of input from our staff. As principal, I was meant to listen to the parent for a bit and then transition the parent or student to the counseling team, which moved into our system for dealing with bullying. I had to stop being a hero and stay focused on my essential work. I knew if a bullying situation became extreme, the counseling team would involve me at the appropriate time. I needed to focus my time on the critical work and build my competence there.

An effective principal will put a system in place so that *if*, most likely *when*, the issue arises again, everyone in the school knows exactly what to do and how to respond. And while you're building systems, be sure to take enough time to get to the root of complex issues within the school environment. It's essential to consider each issue's underlying reasons; solve issues fundamentally, not symptomatically, and try not to move quickly from one task to the next. Rushing often results in finding quick answers and solutions for the current issue's symptoms without addressing the underlying, foundational issues. The issue at hand will continue to emerge. This will pull you from taking action on essential things to dealing with a recurring issue. Effective leaders don't act like the symptom solutions are fixing the fundamental issue. Once you have systems in place, get into the habit of debriefing each of them right after using them. Revising and strengthening these systems will make them even better the next time around.

Building systems creates competence and confidence in your leadership. Your staff members will feel the surety of the organization's structure. And they will simultaneously develop their own capacity. With systems in place, your school is a much healthier place in which to work, and you, as principal, are taking action with grade-level and department teams about what your students are learning.

Let's look at four systems that are critical to establish for your school: (1) the academic core system, (2) the substitute teacher system, (3) the new teacher induction system, and (4) the teacher observation and evaluation system.

Academic Core System

As you review your systems list, the most critical system, the academic core system, should appear at the top. This system is so essential that your principal playbook devotes three pages to it: the ELA, mathematics, and other subjects pages. The goals listed on each page should guide you and your staff into the actions each day that move those goals forward. These pages represent the complex instructional goals of building your academic core system, piece by piece. These goals take intentional work throughout the semester: meeting with your teachers, discussing specific instruction, and reviewing learning data.

You want to make certain your academic core system goals are achieved so your school will be able to move forward with a new set of goals in the upcoming semester. The achievement of these goals goes hand in hand with the achievement of your students. Your academic core system is where you should be taking action daily. You are continually refining and deepening the work of what your students are learning, getting interventions in place for those who are struggling, and accelerating the learning for each and every student. No work is more important.

Substitute Teacher System

At Scribner Middle School, we had many systems to get in place when I began as principal. My focus on being in classrooms was continually disrupted because I was called out to handle issues so often. Quickly, I turned to my systems list and began prioritizing systems to help with these issues. I placed one or two from the list on the other systems page in the principal playbook.

In my first semester, two teachers, our assistant principal, our administrative assistant, and I built our substitute teacher system to help address our school's substitute teacher situation. At the time, we didn't have a process in place for securing subs and getting these important people into the classroom with the information they needed for a successful day. I would receive calls for sub requests during the evening. Then in the morning, I'd have several substitutes standing at my office door, wondering what to do for the day. We needed a system, and quick!

I scheduled a meeting with our assistant principal, administrative assistant, and two teachers to discuss only the topic of substitutes. We talked about every concern, and we mapped out a plan for how teachers would request a substitute for sick days as well as the exact procedure that substitutes would use when they entered our school. I won't go into all the details, but the gist of it was that first, subs went to my administrative assistant, who checked them in and gave them a school badge and our substitute handbook; then fellow teachers or secretarial staff escorted them to their classroom. Teachers prepared an emergency lesson plan that the substitute teacher could pull and use for the day if they had to be out unexpectedly. When teachers returned to school after being out, they would place a new emergency lesson plan in the administrative assistant's file. Most of these emergency lesson plans have become digitalized, and the students continue to get instruction from their teacher even though the teacher is not physically present in the classroom.

Once that system was in place, I was never pulled away to welcome substitutes, find materials for them, or escort them to classrooms to begin the school day. Through the years, I did become involved in creating another aspect of the substitute teacher system for when the school simply didn't have enough substitutes to cover the classrooms. Our leadership team developed a plan and clarified how we would equitably use other teachers and staff members in those situations. For really difficult days with several absent teachers and a shortage of subs, we developed a plan to combine classrooms in the auditorium where our guidance counselors worked with students, using prepared lessons on a few of their guidance standards. This system was in place when the substitute shortage situation occurred. It didn't happen often, but we were ready. Of course, if there was ever a concern with any substitute, I was ready to handle those situations. This system worked and allowed me to gain invaluable time for team meetings and classroom observations, instead of spending critical time each morning getting substitutes in place.

New Teacher Induction System

Another system that went into the principal playbook in my first semester was the new teacher induction system. What an essential system! Anne Watkins (2016), senior director of teacher induction at the New Teacher Center, writes:

> The positive impact of a leader who creates a caring learning community focused on student success is evident to all, including beginning teachers. Research reveals that inadequate support from school administration is one of the three most often reported causes of a new teacher's decision to leave the profession . . . Principals who are knowledgeable about the issues affecting new teachers, proactive in supporting them, and committed to professional growth do make a significant difference. (p. 1)

But our school didn't have a detailed system in place throughout the year for new teachers. This system should include first-year teachers and any teachers new to the building. Our leadership team wanted to consider both these groups. Muhammad (2018) calls first-year teachers Tweeners. He calls brand-new educators Level One Tweeners and educators with prior experience Level Two Tweeners. Muhammad (2018) writes that the first few years these staff members are at your school can be unpredictable but critical years. Principals must help the Tweeners find meaning in their new roles. These new teachers to the school "are blank slates. Administrators who provide these new professionals with proper support can fill that slate with good experiences and drastically change the school culture" (Muhammad, 2018, p. 67).

My middle school's staff and I developed a strong structure to support new teachers, starting with having them visit the school prior to summer break to receive reading material. We developed summer induction days to take place before school began. Over this induction time, usually two full days, we reviewed in detail the pacing guide, common formative assessments, classroom management, and several other topics. We explained the principal playbook and the goals that would affect each of the new teachers. We shared our systems list and those systems we were currently working on. We assigned mentors. The PTO presented these new teachers with school supplies and school wear.

From there, I held monthly meetings to ensure we stayed in close contact and presented each of the new teachers with a journal where they could keep notes throughout the year and share their thoughts in our meetings. We met the first Friday of each month for an hour. We did three things in our time together: (1) discussed a selected topic, like reviewing individualized education plans (IEPs) and 504s; (2) shared entries from their new teacher journals; and (3) closed by ensuring they took with them all the pertinent information for the upcoming month.

By the end of their first year in our school, I had visited their classrooms many times, met with each of them monthly, and discussed their personal journal ideas and concerns. It was critical that I know them as individuals, know their teaching style, and know that they felt supported and connected to our school family and me by the end of their first year. The goal of our new teacher induction program was for new teachers to feel more support, structure, and friendship at our school than they could anywhere else.

Teacher Observation and Evaluation System

Your system of observations and evaluation feedback is one of the most critical you will build. You don't want mediocre and ineffective practices in your school's classrooms. Once-a-semester observations are not effective; lengthy evaluation forms with meaningless comments are not effective; and quick walkthroughs with checklists can be ineffective too. Kim Marshall (2019) suggests that you want your observations and evaluations to result in "more good teaching in more classrooms more of the time. And that is the key to raising the next generation of well-educated Americans and closing our social-class and racial-achievement gaps."

Classroom observations involve so many things. Teachers deserve your focused, undivided attention just as students deserve that of their teachers. Teachers should have a clear understanding of their instructional goals, data that they can use to determine whether students are making progress, and necessary supports to help in achieving goals. Through classroom observations, you can have regular communication with the teacher, set high expectations, individualize the teacher's role in the shared vision, and allocate resources when needed. Through classroom observations, you are trying to create a positive environment for teachers to continually grow in their instructional methods.

Short, frequent, and usually unannounced visits work well for many principals (Marshall, 2019). These frequent visits allow principals to spot mediocre and ineffective practices.

They're about being proactive through your observations, not reactive. Concentrate on observing the strategies and techniques that the teachers, grade level, or department are working on together. Visit often enough to have a solid understanding of what's going on in classrooms so you can provide informative, specific feedback.

After observations, you can follow up with informal coaching. Face-to-face conversations and brief summaries of the visits can be helpful. Discuss the teacher's goals and student learning data a few times throughout the semester. And in the teacher's final evaluation meeting, set aside forty to forty-five minutes for a wrap-up of the current semester's goals and data and the next semester's clear goal setting.

What were the hardest parts for me in finding the time for these invaluable classroom observations and conversations? Two things. First, I had to prepare and plan my schedule to get the observations done each week. Even though I tried to schedule an hour each day for observations and feedback, it was really tough to accomplish. I was trying to attend several grade-level and department meetings, too, to hear teachers discussing data and strategy. So I marked the time in my planner and highlighted it in yellow. Second, I had to maintain the discipline to actually do what I had scheduled. I could not allow other things to take me away from the planned observations. Telling a few teachers that I would be in their classrooms that week seemed to help. When I did that, I was much more determined to make it happen; I wanted to do what I had said I would do.

Manage Time Efficiently

How a school uses time—each minute of the school day—is a significant factor in its success. A school addresses the first two critical questions of a professional learning community (PLC), "What do students need to know and be able to do?" and "How will we know when they have learned it?" (DuFour et al., 2016, p. 251), through pacing guides and common formative assessments. A school addresses the final two critical questions of a PLC, "What will we do when they haven't learned it?" and "What will we do when they already know it?" (DuFour et al., 2016, p. 251), through time management. In order to manage time efficiently, principals should thoughtfully consider three areas: (1) student time, (2) staff time, and (3) their own time.

Student Time

It is of critical importance that principals at all levels—elementary, middle, and high school—spend time getting each student's schedule right before the beginning of the first school day. Effective principals do not leave scheduling to counselors and teachers. They are involved and knowledgeable about students' needs and make certain that schedules meet those needs. They take the necessary time to carefully review student data with teacher leaders, department chairs, and grade-level teachers; initiate placement discussions with teachers when there is a question of the best classroom environment for individual students; and then make knowledgeable and intentional student placement decisions. This scheduling takes place in the spring so that students' reading and achievement levels are as accurate as possible. Students in need of interventions should have them in place on day one of the school year.

Here are a few other items that principals should carefully consider for the best use of students' time.

- Student schedules built and determined around students' particular learning needs

- Literacy interventions embedded in the school day for students not reading at grade level

- Mathematics interventions embedded in the school day for students needing more time with mathematics concepts

- Enrichment time embedded in the school day involving only worthy, challenging, and high-interest opportunities for students who have mastered core content

- Extra tutoring for students after school or before school

As you think through the process of building effective student schedules, keep in mind that the hidden patterns of the school day can profoundly affect students. Daniel Pink (2018), *New York Times* best-selling author of *When: The Scientific Secrets of Perfect Timing*, states that school administrators should have awareness of the peak, trough, and recovery periods for students and plan the instructional day accordingly. Does the time of day for literacy and mathematics instruction matter? Yes! What about the time of day for difficult science and history courses? Yes! Pink shares that cognitive abilities do not remain static over the course of the day. Difficult subject matter, depending on the student, needs to be taught in the morning during the *peak* window. He also reminds readers not to underestimate the power of breaks—for students, teachers, and leaders. He comments that breaks are not a deviation from work; they are part of work (Pink, 2018). I encourage you to keep these things in mind as you engage in the difficult work of creating your students' schedules.

Staff Time

Give special consideration to your staff's time and the way they use every minute of their day. Let's consider these three groups of staff members: (1) teachers, (2) instructional assistants, and (3) noncertified staff.

Teachers

Principals know the importance of teachers having collaborative planning time. High-achieving schools, departments, and grade-level teams have ample time together during the school day along with weekly collaboration time before or after school. The clear expectation for this time together is that teachers discuss the learning needs of their students, review the most current data, establish a priority goal for their current instruction, and then work together to achieve that goal. Some of their work together ties back to making sure they accomplish goals in the principal playbook for the semester.

Teachers' schedules should be intentional, with particular teachers serving particular student needs. If the most effective teacher is needed with the low-performing students, that teacher should be placed there. How many years the teacher has been teaching or has been working at the school doesn't matter. What matters is that students receive the absolute best instruction to meet their needs. Leaders should match teacher strengths and schedules with student needs and schedules. Find and capitalize on the uniqueness of each teacher.

Daily planning time during the school day, weekly collaboration time before or after school, and deliberate pairing of teachers with students are all essential for student achievement.

Instructional Assistants

Effective principals do not overlook the critical role instructional assistants play. Some of the very best ideas for student instruction came from two instructional assistants at our middle school.

These staff members need clear expectations for their daily work. Each of them is an invaluable link in students' learning. You can meet with these assistants individually or in groups to set clear expectations. For instance, your school may need several instructional assistants running guided groups for struggling readers or for small-group mathematics instruction. This is a need at all school levels, not just elementary. You, along with your leadership team, provide specific training for these assistants and meet with them to make certain they feel comfortable and competent with that training. You discuss the students in their care and those students' current reading levels. These assistants discuss the semester goals for their students and the data they will be tracking to monitor growth. This kind of goal setting gives relevance and meaning to the work these instructional assistants do every day in schools.

Make certain you meet with your instructional assistants, whether they are special education aides, Title I aides, or media center aides, twice each semester to set clear responsibilities, clear goals, and clear expectations for student growth coming from their personal work.

Noncertified Staff

Effective principals review the schedules for all adults in the school. The scheduling process requires leaders to make certain that all noncertified staff members know their importance and relevance to the organization. The noncertified staff members who could be involved in this process include your administrative assistant, bookkeeper, receptionist, health aide, lead custodian, and cafeteria manager. Each hour of the noncertified staff members' day should be used as effectively as possible.

You can develop a structure for working with your noncertified staff members. In my second year as principal, I decided that I needed to have a one-on-one discussion with noncertified staff members so I could get to know them even better. I wanted to talk about their specific roles in the school, and set a particular goal for the semester to further improve our school's culture. Some principals may think this seems like extra work each semester on top of everything else, but I found the process to be one of the most valuable and instrumental for school culture. No matter their job in your school, all staff members are working together as a team to achieve the common purpose and shared vision. All your staff members matter and are critical to student achievement, and they deserve to understand their relevance and to measure their results. Remember that you, as principal, want each of your staff members to not feel anonymous, irrelevant, or immeasurable (Lencioni, 2007).

All staff members, including these noncertified staff, deserve to know from the principal—the organization's leader—that they are not anonymous to the leader. People want to clearly understand that the principal knows who they are and a little about their lives and families. I've discovered through my experience that most principals seem to do well in this first area of making sure people do not have feelings of anonymity. But the next two areas, relevance and measurement, involve the principal and assistant principal meeting with people to review their particular responsibilities in the school and, finally, setting a goal for the semester, along with a way to measure that goal. In this way, the results are visible and reported at the end of the semester. All noncertified staff members can gain new interest each semester in seeing exactly where their work matters and being able to support their results with real data.

Let me share an example so you have an idea of what this process looks like. Our middle school had an issue with students going to the health office and hanging out there during class. I became aware of this issue when teachers brought it to my attention in a monthly building committee session. The teachers were concerned about the amount of instructional time students were missing. That committee established a schoolwide expectation that no students were allowed to go to the health office unless they had a pass from their teacher. That eliminated several issues. But we still had several students missing too much class.

When Susan, our health aide, and I met for our goal-setting session, I made her aware of the concern. She knew that she tended to allow students to come to the health office between classes and then stay too long before returning to class. She completely understood that her purpose at school was to help keep our students healthy and in class. She was such a caring person and always able to build relationships with students, but she was aware that some of them had begun using her to get out of class. We set her three-part semester goal: Susan, school health aide, (1) will not allow any student to be admitted into the health office between classes (unless there is an emergency situation); (2) will require each student coming to the health office to have a pass with a teacher signature; and (3) will keep a daily log with student name, health issue, and amount of time spent in the health office.

Susan and I met at the end of each quarter to review her data. I had asked her to keep a tally of the number of students attempting to come to the health office between periods and the number of students coming during class without a teacher-signed pass. Of course, she was also keeping her daily log. We were so pleased at what her data showed. There was a steady and consistent improvement from the implementation day to the end of that semester. And most importantly, our students were back in the classroom.

What I hadn't expected was the way this goal setting and data tracking made Susan feel. She now had more clarity about how vital her role was to our school. She was proud of her dedication to students, but she was even prouder of her ability to support the teachers and make a difference. She began keeping more data than I ever really needed, but I knew she wanted to make certain I saw her impact. Clearly, she was relevant to our school and measured her work to substantiate that relevance.

Make certain your noncertified staff members are and feel relevant and their work is being measured. This is your opportunity to help your staff members imagine and see the possibilities and the difference they can make.

Principal Time

Now let's talk about the principal's time—*your* time. This is where it can be so easy to simply stay busy throughout the school day without taking action on the critical work of student learning. It's one thing to *say* your school is a PLC. It's an entirely different thing to be spending your time building and actually becoming a PLC—and then working at becoming a better and better one each year.

So what kinds are things should you be doing with your time? Remember all the deliberate actions we've already mentioned in the first few chapters of this book: establishing your school's vision story, developing your principal playbook, creating a leadership team that moves the work forward, and building the systems of your school. These actions are necessary for the school to run efficiently so you can spend as much time as possible on learning. If some of your responsibilities do not have much impact on student learning, try to shift those tasks to other members of your staff. Why? Again, so you can focus as much of your time on how students are learning in your school. Yes, that involves classroom observations. But even more important than classroom observations may be your attendance and involvement in the grade-level and department meetings where you assist teachers in focusing on student learning problems revealed by the assessments and analyzing student work samples. Your time is spent with teachers developing timely and specific interventions to accelerate learning. You're demonstrating that you fully embrace the four questions of a PLC and the work that each of them requires within your school.

As principal, you play a vital role in the progress your teachers make in helping students learn better. Being part of the learning data discussions, encouraging teachers to investigate other strategies to implement, and supporting them with any resources they may need are critical. DuFour and his colleagues (2016) put it best when they call on principals to "shift their focus from watching teaching to using the PLC process to monitor learning, to abandon the idea of instructional leadership, and to embrace the idea of principal as lead learner" (p. 247).

In my first year at Scribner, I remember my administrative assistant Barbara asking what to say to people when they called Scribner and wanted to talk with me but I was never in the office much. I thought about my response for a bit and said, "Tell them this: Our principal isn't in the office. She's out in classrooms working with teachers and discussing how our students are learning. Let me try to help you. If you still need to speak with her, I'll leave a message for her when she's out of classrooms. I'm sure she'll get back with you." It was important to me that parents, district office personnel, and our community knew where I was spending my time.

Create a Principal Monthly Guide

As you continue to do the work of achieving your goals on the principal playbook and building your systems from your systems list, another supporting document to consider creating is a principal monthly guide. This tool served as my reminder of the specific things that needed to be done each month. It housed the information of most everything to do in a particular month and exactly when. This principal monthly guide is a basic to-do list and a tool to assist you in not forgetting anything and knowing the exact timing of doing specific tasks each month. It serves a different role than the principal playbook, which is the critical document with your learning priorities and most important work of the whole semester.

During my first year as principal, a fellow administrator at one of the district's high schools shared his principal monthly guide with me. He advised me to start my own guide by jotting down the important tasks for each month on my calendar. He told me to closely review his monthly guide to make certain I hadn't forgotten to place any items on mine. It was such a helpful tool. I began making mine as specific as I could by recording completion dates. That way, I was never left wondering things like, "Now which week did I send that back-to-school letter to staff? And what day last summer did we email student schedules to our parents? And exactly which week in May do the incoming students from each of our nine elementary schools visit our middle school?"

Creating the guide is a very simple process. In a three-column table, list the month in the first column, the tasks to do that month in the second column, and the exact day, date, or specific week to do those tasks in the third column. Just as my friend and fellow administrator did for me, I've provided a generic example of a principal monthly guide to start your thinking and to compare to the tool you might currently be using. See figure 4.1 for a two-month sample; you can visit **go.SolutionTree.com/leadership** for the full version. I've included a few of the national recognition dates in the United States, but it's most critical that you get everything important to you on the guide. Make it your own; for example, some of the tasks in the figure have the date left blank because individual principals will have their own preferences for when to handle them.

Control Your Time

By doing the work of building your systems, managing time efficiently, and creating your principal monthly guide, you can create clarity and consistency around the work of your school.

Principals must spend time on the right work. So be in control of your time. Don't let other things take your time away from being in classrooms, meeting with teachers, and talking with students about their learning. Plan your day with essential work, but don't forget to build in essential margins—blocks of twenty minutes or so where nothing is scheduled—which will allow you to handle the unexpected things that arise. Give yourself those margins. Give yourself enough time to get from one meeting to the next. Give yourself time to handle the stress of the day. It's easy to become emotionally overwhelmed and feel that you're always running out of time. Take action by acting with deliberateness and awareness so you don't cause yourself more turmoil with competing priorities. Margins in your daily schedule are essential. Hopefully, they will help you feel like you have control of your time, instead of it controlling you.

The work of effective principals is complex, difficult, and demanding. Build a daily schedule so you can be the most effective leader possible for your staff and students.

To reflect on taking action instead of being busy and begin work on your next steps, see the reproducible tools on pages 78–81.

Month	Task	Date
July	National Ice Cream Month	
	Meet with all instructional assistants in a group meeting.	Week before school for those who voluntarily attend Second day of school for others
	Lead opening day with teachers	Opening day
	Meet with the safety team.	Opening day (p.m.)
	Facilitate the semester off-site meeting.	First week
	Lead open house night.	First week
	Send the welcome-back letter to staff.	First week
	Begin the new teacher induction program.	First Friday of school
	Do a walkthrough with the lead custodian for final facility preparations.	Second week
	Meet with substitute teachers to review the substitute handbook.	Second week
	Update the school website.	Second week
	Meet with teacher leaders for specifics of the academic core.	
	Review student-teacher strategic scheduling.	
	Finalize student transfer requests.	
	Perform safety drills.	
August	Be Kind to Humankind Week	Last week
	Observe classrooms and teacher instruction sixteen to twenty hours.	Throughout the month
	Attend grade-level and department meetings to observe, listen to, and support teachers.	Throughout the month
	Facilitate picture day.	First week
	Lead the new teacher induction meeting.	First Friday
	Conduct English learner parent night.	Third week
	Plan and lead the monthly faculty meeting.	
	Conduct the school budget review and monitor grants.	
	Meet with all noncertified staff in individual meetings.	
	Begin instruction for students on student-led conferencing.	
	Perform safety drills.	

Figure 4.1: Principal monthly guide excerpt.

Reflection Questions for Managing Time Effectively

Take a few minutes to reflect on the following questions involving your staff's time and schedule at your school. Circle the appropriate number rating for each reflection question, with 1 meaning *needs significant development*, 2 meaning *needs some development*, 3 meaning *effective*, and 4 meaning *super effective* or *a clear strength*. Then write down ideas that come to mind for strengthening time management in that area.

Reflection Question	Rating and Ideas for Better Time Management
Teachers: Have I designed each teacher's schedule to meet the learning needs of students as opposed to the requests and desires of teachers?	1 2 3 4
Teachers: Have I discussed a semester instructional goal with teachers based on their students' learning data and needs?	1 2 3 4
Teachers: Do I hold teachers accountable for monitoring the semester instructional goals by sharing data with student artifacts throughout the semester?	1 2 3 4
Teachers: Have I designed a schedule where teachers meet as departments or grade levels during their planning time once a week?	1 2 3 4
Teachers: Have I designed a way for collaborative teams to meet before or after school once a week?	1 2 3 4
Instructional assistants: Does each instructional assistant have a clear purpose and relevance for student learning in our school?	1 2 3 4
Instructional assistants: Does each instructional assistant have a measurable goal for each semester?	1 2 3 4

Reflection Question	Rating and Ideas for Better Time Management			
Instructional assistants: Do I meet with this group twice each semester to share their instructional goals and accomplishments together?	1	2	3	4
Noncertified staff: Does each noncertified staff member have a clear purpose and relevance in our school?	1	2	3	4
Noncertified staff: Does each noncertified staff member have a measurable goal for each semester?	1	2	3	4
Noncertified staff: Do I meet with all noncertified staff members twice each semester to establish their goals and then review their accomplishments?	1	2	3	4
Principal: Do I spend the majority of my time each week monitoring student learning?	1	2	3	4
Principal: Do I observe classrooms *and* join the grade-level and department meetings where assessment data and student work samples are being analyzed?	1	2	3	4
Principal: Do I assist teachers in developing timely and specific interventions to accelerate student learning?	1	2	3	4
Principal: Do I embrace the four critical questions of a PLC and spend time addressing each of them?	1	2	3	4

Reflection Questions for Managing Time Effectively With Systems

Take a few minutes to reflect on the time you spend building the systems of your school. Read the following questions, and circle the appropriate number rating for each reflection question, with 1 meaning *needs significant development*, 2 meaning *needs some development*, 3 meaning *effective*, and 4 meaning *super effective* or *a clear strength*. Then write down ideas that come to mind for strengthening time management in that area.

Reflection Question	Rating and Ideas for Better Time Management
Systems: Have I prioritized my time to make certain the school's systems are being built and running efficiently? Each semester, am I consistently choosing two to three systems (from my systems list) to create, improve, or strengthen so that I dedicate the majority of my time to instruction and learning?	1　　2　　3　　4
Systems: Do I take the necessary time to use my systems to fundamentally solve issues rather than quickly take care of the issues' symptoms?	1　　2　　3　　4
Academic core system: Do I always prioritize the academic core system each semester to push teacher instruction and student learning forward?	1　　2　　3　　4
Substitute teacher system: Do I have this system in place, running smoothly and effectively?	1　　2　　3　　4
New teacher induction system: Have I created this system—beginning in the summer and running throughout the entire school year—incorporating monthly meetings with me, supportive mentors, and any needed supports and resources for these new teachers?	1　　2　　3　　4
Observation and evaluation system: Do I have a consistent system in place for my classroom walkthroughs and observations? Do I facilitate meaningful conversations and share relevant data in my evaluation sessions with teachers?	1　　2　　3　　4
Principal monthly guide: Have I created my principal monthly guide to help me keep track of systems and other things? Have I created this tool to assist me with a consistent delivery of our school's programs throughout the year?	1　　2　　3　　4

Template for Goal Setting With Noncertified Staff

As mentioned in this chapter, principals strive for each staff member's time to be used in effective and meaningful ways. No staff members want to feel anonymous, irrelevant, or unable to measure their work. Use this template to help document the semester goals you set with your noncertified staff members. This tool can help ensure you really know these vital colleagues, understand the relevancy of their roles in the school tied to semester goals, and can measure their goals to share results at the completion of the semester.

Noncertified Staff Member	Anonymous to Known	Irrelevant to Relevant	Not Measurable to Measurable
Example: Susan, Health Aide	Shared things about her grown children	Susan's semester goal: 1. Students will not be allowed in the health office between classes. 2. Students must have a pass from their teacher to enter the health office. 3. Susan will keep a daily log to track the length of time each student was in the health office.	Results: 1. Susan allowed no students to enter the health office between classes. 2. Susan had all students without a pass (unless it was an emergency situation) return to their classroom to get a pass from their teacher. 3. Susan shared her daily log, reviewed the data, and explained the improvements she had made in the length of time students were out of class.

Source: Adapted from Lencioni, P. (2007). The three signs of a miserable job: A fable for managers (and their employees). San Francisco: Jossey-Bass.

CHAPTER 5

Lead Effective Meetings

The question came from my administrative assistant, Barbara, in my first year as principal. She said, "I'm just the messenger here, but the athletic coaches want to know if they have to attend your after-school faculty meetings. They haven't attended most meetings in the past. What do you want me to tell them?"

Barbara was an incredible administrative assistant and worked diligently to assist me any way she could. She had been in her position for twelve years before I arrived and was usually able to find the positive while juggling all her responsibilities. But not on this particular day. Demanding staff members, angry parents, and a stack of to-do things on her desk had just about pushed her to the limit. The final school bell had rung and all students had cleared the building for the day. Her office had just emptied of several teachers needing things from her. She collapsed into her chair behind her desk just as I came bounding through the door from attending department meetings most of the afternoon.

"What's wrong, Barbara? Has it been rough up here in the office?" I asked.

"That's an understatement," she replied. "It's been so hectic and I've tried to help everyone, but sometimes, it's just too much. We're putting out fires all the time. We've got to get some better systems in place. And please tell the football, dance, and cheerleading coaches what to do about your meetings. They're waiting out in the common area."

"OK," I said as I walked into my office to grab my things for the faculty meeting. My head was spinning. Our leadership team, along with several other staff members, had already begun the work of building our systems. But I knew Barbara was right; as the process of establishing our systems was ongoing, we still had to put bandages on several issues that popped up, knowing that the situations would probably recur until our systems were built and embedded. We had a plan. We were working through our systems list as productively as we could. Now I felt frustrated and a bit angry that the coaches (staff members, not lay coaches) even questioned if they should attend our faculty meetings. Didn't they understand that it was critical for us to meet as a schoolwide team, collaborate, and grow together as a staff? No, they didn't. I realized at that moment that I had to show staff why meetings in our school were meaningful and essential to our progress.

Once you have the principal playbook in place with goals and action steps, it's important that you take a close look at the meetings taking place in your school and the worthiness of each of them. Meetings have come to bear nothing but a poor connotation. Poorly run meetings can consume way too much time in schools and have no real meaning or results. Principals can and need to change that way of thinking so that meetings are positive, worthy, and constructive time together. Principals need to make certain that the right people are invited and involved in the right meetings. My experience has led me to believe that many staff members in schools think meetings are a waste of time. We need to prove them wrong. In fact, Patrick Lencioni (2012) writes:

> No action, activity, or process is more central to a healthy organization than the meeting. As dreaded as the "m" word is, as maligned as it has become, there is no better way to have a fundamental impact on an organization than by changing the way it does meetings. (p. 173)

Leaders have allowed meetings to become meaningless. I've actually heard principals say, "I don't have time to attend meetings. I've got work to get done!" But if leaders effectively use and facilitate the right meetings, those are exactly where the critical and meaningful work gets done.

In this chapter, we will discuss six foundational meetings to ground the work of your school.

1. Daily check-in meeting
2. Weekly office team meeting
3. Topical meeting (as needed)
4. Biweekly leadership team meeting
5. Monthly faculty meeting
6. Semester off-site meeting

Meeting 1: Daily Check-In Meeting

The purpose of this meeting is to pull your office team together for a five-minute, nobody-sits-down meeting. At Scribner Middle School, six staff members would gather in the commons area five minutes after the bell rang for first period to begin. The assistant principal, the three counselors, the school resource officer, and I would use those five minutes to quickly remind one another of any meetings that day, any staff members who were absent, and anything that might have occurred the previous night at a school or athletic event. We stood right there in a circle, quickly debriefed, and then headed off for the day.

I must be totally honest. At first, I thought this might be a waste of time, and I didn't embed this meeting right away. But when I saw my colleague Steve begin facilitating this daily check-in at his large middle school resulting in less confusion and more answered questions from those five minutes together, I was convinced. It became a catalyst for starting our day on a positive note and ultimately saving time throughout the day.

The office team members knew not to schedule any meetings until ten minutes after first period started. If one team member was absolutely needed elsewhere that morning, the other four members and I would go ahead without that member. But as we got used to this daily five-minute meeting and settled into the routine, several things began to happen: we quit corresponding through email as much (both during the day and in the evening); we quit calling each other several times a day for basic information; and we quit using our annoying radios as much to ask questions of each other throughout the day. Instead, we simply saved the information we could share the next morning. Some of us would use sticky notes to jot down anything we wanted to mention in the next daily check-in. We truly began saving time and found ourselves more focused on the essential work of the day.

Instead of searching for a counselor all morning and then figuring out later in the day that the counselors were out of the building, I found out about their absence the day before when a counselor mentioned during the check-in that they'd be out for a district counselor meeting. Instead of finding out that we had several substitute teachers when the calls for assistance started coming into the front office, I found out first thing that morning in our daily check-in and asked our school resource officer to periodically check on specific substitutes. Instead of finding a coach or two at my office door throughout the day to report situations, I had already heard about the situations in the daily check-in and had begun appropriate action. The daily check-in meetings were absolutely worth the five or six minutes first thing in the morning. I wish I'd begun using them much sooner than I did.

Meeting 2: Weekly Office Team Meeting

This is the meeting that helps keep the school running efficiently. It typically lasts an hour and fifteen minutes and involves the same people in the daily check-in with the addition of the administrative assistant—what I refer to as the *office team*. The main purpose of this meeting is to discuss the weekly topics and issues that need to be handled to help systems work smoothly. Often, attendees review the principal monthly guide and the systems list during the meeting to make certain they are addressing all items. Topics in this weekly team meeting almost always include some principal playbook items from the other systems page, involving things like student attendance, registration issues, new student induction, state or provincial testing procedures, counselor discussion on any current concerns, the school resource officer report, discipline issues, parent requests for class changes, cafeteria issues, and so on. The school office team could meet in the principal's office or the front office conference room. A large whiteboard is a useful tool to have in the room where your school office team meets.

For these meetings, there is no set agenda. Lencioni (2012) explains that in this kind of meeting, "instead of putting together an agenda ahead of time, team members need to come together and spend their first ten minutes of [the] meeting creating a real-time agenda" (p. 179). Create your real-time agenda by taking the following steps.

1. Begin with two to three minutes of sharing about any important topics or concerns the team needs to know about for this particular week.

2. Ask each team member to share only one or two top work priorities or concerns for the upcoming week or two. Each team member gets one minute, enough time to summarize but not go into great detail. This process is called

the *lightning round*. It is your responsibility to hold your team members to the time limit and not allow someone to ramble on and hijack the process.

3. Take brief, bulleted notes as each team member speaks.

4. Quickly review your brief notes to help determine the topic or two for the team to discuss in detail. These topics will become an action plan that the team will create in the time remaining. Select items that you can discuss and finalize in that same meeting.

5. After discussing the topic, select a team member to write down the action steps on the whiteboard, using the same basic template as found in the principal playbook. The team member then adds a fifth column and lists in it any other topics from the lightning round that need further discussion. Then the team decides whether to discuss those items in the next weekly office team meeting or to schedule a topical meeting. Figure 5.1 shows an example of a completed action plan.

Who	What	By When	Metric	Other Items
Counselors	Develop a grade-level testing schedule for initial review.	Next Tuesday	Copies of testing schedules for each grade level	Special education IEP paperwork deficiencies— topical meeting
School resource officer	Create a proposal for the suggested eighth-grade cadet program.	Next Tuesday	Copies of the proposal	Assessment technology concerns— topical meeting
Assistant principal	Problem solve and bring two to three options for seventh-grade cafeteria seating issues.	This Friday	Two to three options	
Eighth-grade counselor	Share (with Rhonda) a list of interested staff for the voluntary discussion of "103 Things White People Can Do for Racial Justice" (Shutack, 2017)	This Friday	The list	

Figure 5.1: Weekly office team meeting action plan.

Visit go.SolutionTree.com/leadership for a free reproducible version of this figure.

When you close a meeting with a concrete action plan, it is clear who's going to do what by when. When the next week's meeting begins, team members know their team will hold them responsible for having their actions completed. This makes the consistency of the work much better. Team members clearly realize that they depend on one another to get their parts done so the team can move forward with the next topic. If team members don't complete their work in the action plan, they hamper the team's process. Making excuses and not showing up are unacceptable. If team members don't fulfill their responsibilities, then you must have follow-up conversations as to why they aren't doing so and what can be done to make things right. Members of the team count on you to hold people accountable in the beginning. But the process should evolve to the point where team members ultimately hold each other accountable.

There is a final aspect to discuss regarding this weekly office team meeting. Often, principals gain awareness of instances where staff members feel like they don't know what's going on at school. Important information is not reaching them. The principal and team members must communicate consistent and clear messages to every person on staff. If teachers come to you asking questions and looking for the exact information that you discussed in the weekly office team meeting a few days earlier, that means there isn't clear communication. When this happened to me, I got really upset. I'd go to the team members and ask why they hadn't shared all the information with the people they represented. They would respond with answers like, "Well, I was going to share everything in our regular department meeting on Friday. You didn't give us a deadline, did you?" or "Oh, I didn't really think that information was important to tell everyone about."

One specific situation that brought everything to a head in our middle school was the week my school office team was discussing our state assessment plans. It was my second year as principal and our counseling team had worked with me to have every detail lined out: specific times for each grade level's testing, room locations, instructional assistant assignments, special accommodations rooms for extra time, snack schedules, teacher manuals, and so on. It was critical that every teacher and instructional assistant know the details of the testing plan. I felt great about our work as a school office team and was proud of the detailed planning to make the assessment process go as smoothly as possible for everyone. I felt great until Monica, a physical education teacher, walked up to me on the morning of testing and asked me if she could help out in any way since she didn't have any students to test.

"What?" I asked.

"Well, I know testing starts this morning, and I was just wondering if you had scheduled me to help out anywhere. What should I do while students test this morning?"

My heart sank. I was terrified that if Monica didn't know the school office team had assigned her to a particular group of students to test, other teachers also didn't know their assignments. I panicked. A real big panic! I went running to our sixth-grade counselor to see why Monica didn't know she had a group of students to begin testing in about thirty minutes. The team member went into a long explanation that Monica had been absent a couple of days the previous week and the information was just never communicated. The team member was on the way to give Monica all her testing materials and explain everything quickly. What a mess!

That was not acceptable. Monica was always willing to help, and our new sixth-grade counselor simply got a bit overwhelmed with all the testing requirements. I quickly realized I needed a system for meeting closure where we, the office staff team, determined the exact information to share and a specific timeline for communicating that information. I was living the horror of what happens when team members don't "stop and clarify what they've agreed to and what they will go back and communicate to their teams" (Lencioni, 2012, p. 187). So when it came time to end our meetings, the last five to six minutes would consist of answering three questions.

1. *What* have we decided today that we need to share with others?

2. Exactly *when* will we share this information?

3. *How* will we share this information?

The following sections cover how to answer each of these questions as a team.

What Have We Decided Today That We Need to Share With Others?

Ask this question, and make a list of things that team members need to share with other staff. Use a whiteboard for this purpose if you have one. Team members should jot these items down too. If the team has nothing that needs to be shared, make it clear that there is no information to share with other staff. If there is information to share, move to the second question.

Exactly When Will We Share This Information?

You lead the team in determining when the information needs to be shared—that same day, the next day, or later in the week. Get as specific as you can. Your team may decide, "We will share this information on Wednesday, anytime after one o'clock but before school is out for the day."

I can't begin to tell you how much this helped the school run more efficiently. Teachers felt much better informed, and information got to people at as close to the same time as possible. It became rare for any teacher to come to me with questions about things our school office team members and I had determined to share as a team. But again, the principal is responsible for holding the team members accountable in any instance when they do not get the information out appropriately. It's a critical part of being a healthy organization.

When I served as director of middle schools in my district, I worked very closely with the directors of elementary and high schools. After our weekly cabinet meetings with the superintendent, we directors would almost always have information to share with building principals. One director was the absolute quickest to disseminate information. Sometimes the information would travel to building principals at all levels—elementary, middle, and high school—before I could even get back to my office following the cabinet meeting. The other director and I would certainly get the information out, but it might be the next day. You can imagine how this worked for all three of us. Phone calls from middle school principals started rolling in at my office.

"Rhonda, why don't we know anything about this?" principals would ask. They'd be upset or concerned that they didn't know important information. It became clear that the three of us, as district directors for elementary, middle, and high schools, had to agree on when we were going to share information with principals. Once we got on the same page, there was a much smoother and more efficient communication system. Information cascaded to the sixteen schools in our district much more efficiently. It was only fair to all our administrators that they hear the same messages at approximately the same time. The three of us got much better at doing this, and it certainly was better for our principals.

How Will We Share This Information?

Do you want to send an email with the information, see people in person, make phone calls, send a text, or what? You need to make the means of communicating the information explicitly clear to your team members. Each piece of information may need to use a different mode of communication, depending on the exact topic. If you're sharing information about an upcoming faculty meeting, for example, an email would work. If you're reviewing the details of the upcoming state testing schedule with staff responsibilities, an in-person meeting might feel best. If you need to ask a staff member to chaperone the dance next Friday, a phone call or text gets it done quickly. If you're sharing sensitive information with a staff member, showing up for a conversation face to face might be necessary.

Meeting 3: Topical Meeting

What are topical meetings, and why are they necessary? A *topical meeting* is one in which only one topic is discussed. There are two reasons to have topical meetings. The first reason is to focus on a topic that is going to take concentrated time and effort to solve and create an action plan for. Let's use the earlier example of state or provincial testing. You can schedule an hour-and-a-half meeting to focus on the logistics, scheduling of computer labs, snack breaks, special education accommodations, specific updates from the testing manual, and all other concerns for the upcoming testing. When a counselor brings up the state or provincial testing in the weekly office team meeting, you don't have to discuss it at that time. That topic deserves a separate meeting where you'll have enough time to discuss all the testing issues and actually get a plan in place.

The second reason for a topical meeting is to make certain you have all the essential people in the meeting. For instance, in the state or provincial assessment topical meeting, you may need a few teachers and technical support staff to join you and the counselors. Whenever you schedule a topical meeting and invite staff members, always ask them to come prepared with a few problem-solving ideas in mind to share at the meeting.

Before the office team members and I began using topical meetings, we spent some of our weekly office team meeting time discussing too many of these more involved topics. It felt like no sooner did we begin tossing around ideas than our time was up. It was so frustrating. And often, we never got back together to solve the issue entirely. Team members went their own way and worked on a few items on their own, and when they came back the next week, we were in pretty much the same place as the week before. You'll notice in figure 5.1 (page 86), the weekly office team meeting action plan, that two topical meetings appear in the last column (Other Items): (1) special education IEP paperwork deficiencies and (2) assessment technology concerns. Both of those topics came up in the weekly office team meeting, and we knew we would not have adequate time or the needed staff members to address them completely.

Once you've had a focused and intentional meeting on a single topic, you should be able to create a solid and effective plan with the fundamental solutions to most of the concerns. Our office team's first topical meeting on state testing took several hours for us to get a complete, systematic plan in place for the school's testing. But every year after, when that topic came up in our office team meeting, we simply planned an hour or so for a topical meeting where we reviewed our system for testing. We spoke with our district assessment director, who shared any new information and details we needed for that year and answered our questions. Once we had all our needed information, we made the necessary adjustments and revisions.

Topical meetings are a necessary part of getting issues addressed and solutions ready to embed into your school. Once you embed these meetings into your school's culture, you'll immediately feel the efficiency of them. And remember to bring closure to the meetings by asking the three clarifying questions for cascading communication appropriately.

Meeting 4: Biweekly Leadership Team Meeting

This team meeting is the critical meeting where the curricular needs of your school are addressed. This meeting is where discussion of your core purpose—student learning and rigorous instruction—takes place.

Members who attend the biweekly leadership team meetings include the staff the principal has selected with the process discussed in chapter 3 (page 51). These are the people driving the work of the principal playbook; they make their decisions in the best interest of the entire school, not their particular department or grade level. These team members must understand that they are part of this critical team to become informed about all aspects of learning in the school. They are on this team and in these meetings to inquire about all aspects of teaching in your school, to fully understand the academic priorities, and to advocate for what they believe is best for the school—even if it's not the easiest thing for their particular area.

The lightning round (page 86), once again, is useful in the leadership team meeting. Begin with a few minutes of important curricular updates, and share any new information from the district office. Then team members go around the table, sharing information from the department or grade level they represent and focusing their comments on action steps from the principal playbook goals.

After the lightning round, select one or two topics that you can discuss and solve in the meeting's remaining time. Then you can place items on a whiteboard for the next leadership team meeting or any necessary topical meetings. Just as in the weekly office team meetings, close the meeting with the three clarifying questions. Once the curricular work of the school is running efficiently, the principal might facilitate this meeting every three weeks or even once a month, as long as the academic initiatives are moving forward and the team is well informed of the work throughout the school. The principals I've worked with have found this frequency to work well.

Meeting 5: Monthly Faculty Meeting

Small groups of your staff are meeting regularly in department and grade-level team meetings, during planning periods, and in before- and after-school meetings. Effective principals also pull their entire staff together once a month for the sole purpose of building community by being together in one room and highlighting exceptional curricular pieces of the school. This meeting is not about sharing day-to-day information; it's about building the knowledge base and capacity of the entire staff. And, just as important, it's about bonding as a whole staff.

Each month, you can have a one-hour faculty meeting with three basic components: (1) positive reflection, (2) curricular highlight, and (3) closing motivation. First, begin with a few positive minutes to share great things going on at the school, especially with specific work and actions from staff members. At Scribner, this positive reflection involved our mascot, represented by a ceramic panther. I usually began our July opening day sessions by making a few comments about a particular teacher who had done something really spectacular over the summer, and that teacher would receive the panther to display in the classroom for the month. Maybe I highlighted a unit piece a teacher had developed over the summer. One time, a teacher had done extraordinary mentoring of a first-year teacher over the entire summer so the new teacher was ready to go on day one with all the units, assessments, and projects for the first semester. Another time, I gave the ceramic panther to a teacher who had shown incredible kindness and patience while working the school's registration table, where she had assisted parents in completing the free and reduced-price lunch forms. In the next faculty meeting, the keeper of the panther would choose someone else deserving of our dear mascot and pass it on. The giving teacher was required to share the story and specific actions of what the receiving teacher had done to deserve our Scribner panther. I really loved the first few minutes of our faculty meetings because the "panther moment" reflections seemed to always involve something I was unaware of as the leader. It was grounding to hear about these wonderful acts of goodness. That ceramic panther was chipped, lackluster, and missing a pretty big chunk of one ear, but it was a cherished piece of displayed art in our school.

The second faculty meeting component, involving a curricular highlight, takes thirty to forty minutes. This curricular highlight is one area that you want all staff members to know about. It's typically something taken right out of the principal playbook where teachers are doing critical, difficult work with students. Usually, you'll know the area to highlight from all the discussion in the grade-level and department meetings or the leadership team meetings. Some example highlights I used include eighth-grade teachers running guided groups for struggling readers, mathematics teachers presenting student work examples from problem-solving posters, an exceptionally engaging scenario from the seventh-grade science unit that quarter, and the unbelievable guitar unit from the general music class.

The third and final component of the monthly faculty meeting takes only five or six minutes. It's a simple, motivational closing moment. You can share a personal story or example of a faculty member doing above-and-beyond work. Using this component, you know you'll have an opportunity to share every single month about the exceptional things you observe at your school. Sometimes, you'll share about teachers. Other times, you'll share about instructional assistants or members of the custodial team and ask those people to stay for the meeting that afternoon. These stories can motivate your staff to continue working hard, working together, and bringing the vision into reality.

A few other strategies I've learned from colleagues that you might want to incorporate for faculty meetings include the following.

- Start on time—always.

- Share as much information electronically (email, video clip, and so on) outside the meeting as possible. This way you avoid taking up time during the meeting for any clear-cut items that simply need to be shared.

- Provide food, if possible. Scribner's PTO dropped off snacks each faculty meeting day. Staff members brought their own drink and then picked up a snack from a cart placed outside the classroom door on their way into the meeting.

- Meet in classrooms. Scribner used to squish nearly sixty staff members into a classroom, using folding chairs around the perimeter of the room. The host teacher would quickly share one or two things about the classroom, and all staff could see student work displays and other things. Visit exceptional classrooms in the first two months of the school year. Then schedule your next faculty meeting in a teacher's room that could use some sprucing up. By the time the meeting takes place, things will probably show lots of improvement without you ever saying a word!

- End on time.

Meeting 6: Semester Off-Site Meeting

The last of the six meetings embedded into a school's culture is the semester off-site meeting. This meeting plays an essential part in tackling the school's strategic challenges. It takes a full day (or at least four hours) of planning together, but the amount of time saved over the long haul by getting everyone aligned and moving in the same direction can be such a payoff. These meetings should be an exciting and uplifting time together.

Invite your school's leadership team and office team to the off-site meetings. The goal of the semester off-site meeting is to review the prior semester's principal playbook: all the accomplishments from each page as well as any items not fully completed. Attendees of the off-site meeting spend time looking ahead to the goals and action steps for the upcoming semester. It's a time to stop, reflect, and truly celebrate all the work, systems, and progress made. It's a time to have open and honest conversations about some of the difficult work being accomplished at your school. It's a time to catch the essential pieces you didn't get completed and make sure those pieces get placed on the next semester's principal playbook. It's a time of revisiting and revisions. It's a time to review the school's mission. It's a time to review the vision. It's a time to experience a unique setting, getting away from the school. It's a time for a fresh perspective. It's a time to eat together. It's a time to give out silly awards. It's a time to laugh together. It's a time for you, as the school's leader, to thank your team and to show gratitude. It's a time to motivate your team for the work that lies ahead. It's a time to once again focus and clarify. These meetings, twice a year, are critical to the health of your school.

Scribner usually held these semester off-site meetings in July and January. In July, we would hold a full-day meeting three to four weeks before school started. We determined that date before we left for the school year in May or June. Our January meeting would usually be for several hours at night in the first week of our return to school after winter break. We used several locations over the years—the living room of my house, the outdoor porch of an English teacher's home, a basement room of our district office, a private room at a local bank, and our own school's cafeteria (the Panther Porch). I don't recommend that last one. These meetings are much better when you're away from your school. If you have the possibility of using a retreat center or state park for an overnight visit, that would be incredible. Funding from a local sponsor paid for our meals and snacks. And don't forget to close out this sixth and final meeting by asking the three clarifying questions.

1. *What* have we decided today that we need to share with others?

2. Exactly *when* will we share this information?

3. *How* will we share this information?

Meetings Can Matter

As the principal, you own the responsibility of making sure all meetings are an effective use of your and your staff's time. Make meetings something your staff members look forward to and would never want to miss. Stay knowledgeable about your local mandates for school meetings, and work within those parameters. Effective meetings allow you and your school to stay focused on the essential work.

To reflect on leading effective meetings and begin work on your next steps, see the reproducible tools on pages 94–98. And turn to page 99 for a tool to help you reflect on and determine next steps for all of part 1.

Six Meetings Checklist

Take time to reflect on the meetings you currently lead in your school. Then use the following template to check off the boxes once you have answered each of the questions for each meeting type. This is your opportunity to give serious consideration to making meetings meaningful in your school.

Daily Check-In Meeting
☐ Where will this meeting be held?
☐ What specific time will we use for this five-minute meeting?
☐ Who is expected to attend?

Weekly Office Team Meeting
☐ Where will this meeting be held? (Is a whiteboard available?)
☐ What day or time will this meeting be held each week?
☐ Who will be attending this meeting?
☐ Am I ready to begin the meeting with pertinent information, facilitate the lightning round, and then create a real-time agenda?
☐ Jot down items you'll be able to discuss during the meeting, and begin discussion to create action steps for each item.
☐ List other items to be discussed in next week's office team meeting.
☐ List items that require a topical meeting. Make certain to set dates, meeting times, and needed individuals to attend any topical meeting listed.
☐ Am I ready to end with the three clarifying questions?

Topical Meeting
☐ Where will this meeting be held?
☐ How much time is needed for this topic? (Reminder: only this topic is to be discussed.)
☐ Who are the key people to be in attendance for this particular topic?
☐ What specific pieces of information and data are needed for this topical meeting?
☐ Who will be responsible for providing and bringing each piece of information or data to the meeting?
☐ If information is needed before this meeting, by what deadline will this information or data be sent to all attendees?
☐ Am I ready to end with the three clarifying questions?

Biweekly Leadership Team Meeting
☐ Where will this meeting be held? (Is a whiteboard available?)
☐ What day or time will this meeting be held every other week?
☐ Who will be attending this meeting?
☐ Am I ready to begin the meeting with pertinent information, facilitate the lightning round, and then create a real-time agenda?
☐ Jot down items you'll be able to discuss during the meeting, and begin discussion to create action steps for each item.
☐ List other items to be discussed in the next leadership team meeting.
☐ List items that require a topical meeting. Make certain to set dates, meeting times, and needed individuals to attend any topical meeting listed.
☐ Am I ready to end with the three clarifying questions?

Monthly Faculty Meeting
☐ Are monthly dates set for these meetings and given to teachers or staff on opening day?
☐ Have room locations been set for the semester? Or year? (These are not to be shared with staff until they need the meeting room location for the current month.)
☐ Have monthly dates been given to the plant operator (or appropriate staff member) so this staff member can have extra chairs and any other needed furniture set up for meeting?
☐ Is the parent-teacher organization able to provide snacks for each monthly meeting? If not, determine other possibilities.
☐ Am I sharing as much information electronically as possible so that distributing the information does not take critical time from this meeting?
☐ If attendees need to read or listen to information prior to the meeting, have I prepared this information and sent it to staff so they have appropriate time to read or listen to the material?
☐ Am I ready to begin the meeting on time and quickly have the host teacher welcome staff to the classroom?
☐ Is last month's selected teacher ready to share the positive reflection activity for the month and share a personal story about a particular staff member? That staff member will share the following month.
☐ Have I selected the curricular or academic highlight and asked teachers to be ready to present and share?
☐ Am I prepared to share a closing motivation to end the meeting?

Semester Off-Site Meeting
☐ Have meeting dates been set for July and January?
☐ Have leadership team and office team members been invited?
☐ Has an off-site location been selected with specific times?
☐ Have food and snack preparations been made?
☐ Am I ready to lead visioning (either creating a new vision or revising an existing vision)?
☐ Am I ready to review the prior semester's principal playbook accomplishments?
☐ Am I ready to share the upcoming semester's principal playbook with goals and then open discussion for revisions and additions?
☐ Are fun team-building activities planned for throughout the day—the beginning, middle, and end of the meeting?
☐ Am I ready to end with the three clarifying questions?

Six Meetings Review Chart With Notes

Take a look at the bulleted points for each meeting in the following template, and then write your thoughts in the space provided for any action steps you may need.

Daily Check-In Meeting

- Meet for five minutes immediately after students begin class.
- Stand up outside the main office area.
- Do a quick check of information needed for the day.

Notes for Daily Check-In Meeting:

Weekly Office Team Meeting

- Meet for sixty to seventy-five minutes with a real-time agenda.
- Begin with critical weekly information.
- Facilitate the lightning round with team members.
- Select topics for discussion for the remainder of the meeting.
- Designate any topical meetings, if needed.
- Close with the three clarifying questions.
  - a. What have we decided today that we need to share with others?
  - b. Exactly when will we share this information?
  - c. How will we share this information?

Notes for Weekly Office Team Meeting:

Topical Meeting

- Meet for a number of minutes dependent on the topic.
- Discuss one topic only.
- Ensure relevant people are in attendance and bring needed information and data.
- Report results of this meeting in the leadership team and school office team meetings.
- Close with the three clarifying questions.
  - a. What have we decided today that we need to share with others?
  - b. Exactly when will we share this information?
  - c. How will we share this information?

Notes for Topical Meeting:

Biweekly Leadership Team Meeting

- Meet for sixty to ninety minutes with a real-time agenda.

- Begin with critical information.

- Facilitate the lightning round with team members.

- Choose topics to discuss for the remainder of the meeting.

- Designate any topical meetings, if needed.

- Close with the three clarifying questions.

    a. What have we decided today that we need to share with others?

    b. Exactly when will we share this information?

    c. How will we share this information?

Notes for Biweekly Leadership Team Meeting:

Monthly Faculty Meeting

- Meet for sixty minutes.

- Begin with a positive reflection. (Ten minutes)

- Spend meaningful time on a curricular or academic highlight. (Thirty-five to forty minutes)

- Share a closing motivation. (Ten minutes)

Notes for Monthly Faculty Meeting:

Semester Off-Site Meeting

- Meet for four hours to a full day.

- Create or revise the vision.

- Review the principal playbook.

- Engage in team-building activities.

- Close with the three clarifying questions.

    a. What have we decided today that we need to share with others?

    b. Exactly when will we share this information?

    c. How will we share this information?

Notes for Semester Off-Site Meeting:

Self-Rating Scale for Meetings

After several weeks of working toward implementation of the six meeting types, use the following template to self-rate exactly how your meetings are progressing by placing checkmarks in the appropriate spaces.

Meeting	Consistent Implementation	Approaching Consistent Implementation	Average Implementation	Sporadic Implementation	Marginal or No Implementation
Daily Check-In					
Weekly Office Team					
Topical					
Biweekly Leadership Team					
Monthly Faculty					
Semester Off-Site					

Part 1 Final Reflection and Next Steps: Essential Leadership Actions—Be Deliberate!

As a culminating reflection exercise for part 1, take time to review each of the essential leadership actions in the following template to see whether each action is in the beginning stages (Gassing Up!), intermediate stages (Cruising Along!), or final stages (Arrived at Destination!) of implementation. Place a checkmark if you're currently in one of the first two columns. Then write a date in the last column when you've reached full implementation. Mark the areas you will prioritize for strengthening your leadership and for taking deliberate action in moving things forward in your school.

Essential Leadership Actions	Gassing Up! *(Thinking of ideas and processing things)*	Cruising Along! *(Making progress with implementation)*	Arrived at Destination! *(Reached full implementation)* Enter completion date.
Action 1: Establish a Vision Focused on Learning			
Why do we exist? answered			
Academic core components reviewed			
Vision story established			
Action 2: Clarify the Essential Work			
Comprehensive inventory exercise completed			
Systems list created			
Principal playbook developed			
Action 3: Create Teams to Move the Work Forward			
Leadership team developed and in place			
Current and aspiring positive descriptors selected			
Teacher leader team developed and in place			
Action 4: Take Action Instead of Being Busy			
Systems from the systems list prioritized and being created			
Consistency established in solving issues fundamentally			
Student time managed efficiently			
Teacher time managed efficiently			
Instructional assistant time managed efficiently			
Noncertified staff time managed efficiently			

Essential Leadership Actions	Gassing Up! (Thinking of ideas and processing things)	Cruising Along! (Making progress with implementation)	Arrived at Destination! (Reached full implementation) Enter completion date.
Action 4: Take Action Instead of Being Busy (continued)			
Principal's own time managed efficiently			
Principal monthly guide created			
Action 5: Lead Effective Meetings			
Daily check-in meetings implemented			
Weekly office team meetings implemented • Lightning round • Real-time agenda • Closing questions			
Topical meetings implemented • Closing questions			
Biweekly leadership team meetings implemented • Lightning round • Real-time agenda • Closing questions			
Monthly faculty meetings implemented • Positive reflection on a staff member • Curricular or academic highlight • Closing motivation by the principal			
Semester off-site meetings implemented • Vision review and creation • Principal playbook review and creation • Team-building activities			

Essential Leadership Skills

In part 1 (page 9), I shared the story of the Principal of the Year banquet where I sat at a banquet table, feeling like a fraud. Fast-forward a few years. This time, I sat at a university conference room table, defending my dissertation. My dissertation chair, Todd Whitaker, sat across from me. He had carefully led me through the doctoral process, guided each of my steps, and strengthened my belief in the research process. And then that ever-present sentence from the awards banquet came out again—but with a twist this time. I shared with my dissertation committee members that for the first time in my career, I did not feel like an imposter. I now felt equipped to confidently and skillfully lead. The research helped me fully understand the essential leadership actions necessary for effective principals to lead high-achieving schools. But it also helped me understand that effective leadership takes more than these essential actions.

Part 1's five actions are not a simple checklist to introduce to your staff and mark off your list. These actions alone do not ensure a healthy school with high achievement. But when principals use the essential leadership actions with the essential leadership skills presented in part 2, real change can occur. These skills enable principals to engage with people and accomplish the critical work of school improvement. It's one thing to know and understand the essential leadership actions; it's an entirely different thing to have the capacity to work with people and actually turn those actions into real accomplishments. These skills can be hard to develop, but the payoff is immense. Your work in developing these skills demonstrates to your staff that for you, as Sinek shares, leadership "is not about being in charge; it's about taking care of the people in your charge" (as cited in Inspiritory, 2017).

Although it's sometimes difficult to articulate, there is a uniqueness in high-achieving schools where principals lead with competence and care. These schools have a different essence: an intentional, not-by-accident, caring, structured, and efficient way of leading a learning organization. These schools reach new heights of accomplishment yet are always aware of the continual need to improve together.

These schools have the uniqueness of combining an effective principal with empowered teachers. These principals are keenly aware that their leadership skills should lift the organization. This lifting involves principals building and strengthening the essence of their school through compassionate work on themselves and with their staff and students. They create the kind of environment where people want to work, want to be on teams together, and never want to leave.

Most principals want healthier schools. But many do not fully understand that these leadership skills, sometimes referred to as *soft skills*, are not secondary to the leadership actions. These leadership skills take a tremendous amount of time and effort to embed within a school, and this can be exhausting. It's also hard to measure leadership skills; they focus on the more emotional and behavioral aspects of the work and therefore are more subjective. For that reason, principals will often want other staff members to handle these so-called *softer* tasks. That's a mistake. Principals need to lead by example in areas like building relationships, reframing conflict, and holding others accountable. Principals must be the first to do the hardest things. People want to work in a school and stay in a school where the environment is healthy. It's the principal's responsibility to create such an environment.

That's what part 2 is all about. It's about understanding the importance of having these leadership skills to create a healthy school. The skills that served you well as a teacher might not guarantee your success as a principal. Digital media educator Lauren Landry (2019) writes:

> If you aspire to be in a leadership role, there's an emotional element you need to consider. It's what helps you successfully coach teams, manage stress, deliver feedback, and collaborate with others. It's called emotional intelligence, and accounts for nearly 90 percent of what sets high performers apart from peers with similar technical skills and knowledge.

What the research and numbers clearly indicate is that principals cannot become top leaders without emotional intelligence. Goleman (2019) writes that from his research analysis:

> Emotional intelligence proved to be twice as important as the [other capabilities] for jobs at all levels . . . emotional intelligence played an increasingly important role at the highest levels of the company, where differences in technical skills are of negligible importance. In other words, the higher the rank of a person considered to be a star performer, the more emotional intelligence capabilities showed up as the reason for his or her effectiveness . . . In short, the numbers are beginning to tell us a persuasive story about the link between a company's success and the emotional intelligence of its leaders. And just as important, research is also demonstrating that people can, if they take the right approach, develop their emotional intelligence. (pp. 9–11)

The good news is that anyone can develop emotional intelligence skills. You can learn to better understand and manage your own emotions, as well as recognize and influence the emotions of the people who work with you. Principals can learn to build better relationships, control their reactions, practice empathy, and resolve conflict. It's all about building a culture where people want to work and grow.

The essential leadership actions from part 1 (page 9) are capacity-building tools. Alone, each of them can have a positive effect on teaching and learning. But you have to use these actions alongside the essential leadership skills in part 2. Part 1 was all about getting outcomes through your actions; part 2 is all about nurturing people through your skills. Principals must understand that these skills not only distinguish them as outstanding leaders but also establish their ability to demonstrate strong performance.

The work of leading schools is complex and complicated. It requires principals to take both the essential leadership actions and the essential leadership skills and use them throughout their leadership. I have no doubt that no work is more important. But in order to lead a school with these essential skills, be ready to lead with courage. As Brené Brown (2018) writes:

> I want to live in a world with braver, bolder leaders, and I want to be able to pass that kind of world on to my children. I define a leader as anyone who takes responsibility for finding the potential in people and processes, and who has the courage to develop that potential. From corporations, nonprofits, and public sector organizations to governments, activist groups, schools, and faith communities, we desperately need more leaders who are committed to courageous, wholehearted leadership and who are self-aware enough to lead from their hearts, rather than unevolved leaders who lead from hurt and fear. (p. 4)

Let's determine to become more self-aware and more aware of the needs of the people who work with us. Let's determine to intentionally build a culture where everyone feels safe to bring their unique, best self to school. The five essential leadership skills that brave, courageous principals need to hone are:

1. Build relationships
2. Reframe conflict
3. Hold people accountable
4. Lean into the positive
5. Turn inward

I'll discuss each in detail in the following chapters.

CHAPTER 6
Build Relationships

All the essential leadership actions—establishing a vision, clarifying the work, creating teams, taking action, and leading effective meetings—amount to nothing without healthy relationships with the people who work with you. With ever-changing standards and expectations for teachers and staff, you must be a person who empowers other people to grow. And people don't grow without solid relationships with their leader. The achievement gains and progress of your school depend on how well you cultivate each relationship by being consciously aware and intentional in that work.

In this chapter, we will look at three measures to keep in mind as you build relationships with your staff members: (1) build trust, (2) have difficult conversations, and (3) ensure your people find meaning in their work.

Build Trust

As you ask your staff members to perform more challenging and complex work, the ability to build relationships with them becomes more important than ever. And the cornerstone of building relationships is trust. When you create a work environment of trust, you're creating an atmosphere of emotional safety. "People in high-trust relationships communicate well, don't second-guess one another, understand why they are doing things, and are willing to go the extra mile" (Hoff, 2020).

Jim Knight (2017) conducted a study asking staff members to rank the elements of character, competence, reliability, warmth, and stewardship in order of importance for modeling by their building principal. Surprising to many administrators, warmth (which I define as displaying empathy and vulnerability with staff members) outranked competence. Teachers in the research study craved warmth from their leader first, before they could fully consider the leader's competence. Many leaders have great difficulty in showing vulnerability with staff. But it is clear that staff members need to see you as human, feel a connection with you as their leader, and trust that you will be honest, be open, and have their best interests at heart.

Vulnerability doesn't come after trust. It comes before trust. When you're willing to be honest and open about things with your staff, you begin to spark cooperation. Saying things

Handwritten margin notes:
Be intentional and consciously aware in cultivating relationships with other people.

Create an atmosphere of emotional safety by building trust.

Warmth is displaying empathy and vulnerability with staff members
Show your vulnerability
Show you are human
Connect with others
Be honest be open and have the best interest of others at heart.

like, "This is a complex project; we need to work together because I really need help," sends a clear message that you can't do things by yourself and that you need your staff. Being vulnerable involves so many skills: acknowledging what you don't know, apologizing when you make a mistake, trying to fix things when they don't go as planned, giving credit where it is due, not bad-mouthing other people, and consistently showing that you're learning right alongside your staff. When you display vulnerability with your staff, it creates an environment where they feel safe enough to say things like, "I don't know what I'm doing," or "I need some help," or "I made a mistake." You're a strong enough leader to know that when teachers are struggling, you look at your leadership first to make certain you're providing what they need to be successful. If you don't work to create this environment where you and your staff can be open with each other, you have a culture Simon Sinek describes as being full of "lies, hides, and fakes" (as cited in Inspiritory, 2017).

I will never forget a new principal who, at her opening day with staff, said, "I've been so nervous about our first meeting together today. I haven't slept much, but here we go! I'm so excited to be here. I've been working extremely hard to have things prepared as we move this school forward." Those simple but real words resonated with her staff. She was being open and vulnerable right from the start.

In a separate situation, I worked with a principal who didn't have the required curricular units ready to send to the district office by the deadline. He called his leadership team together and said, "I've messed up. I thought we had more time to complete our work on the curricular units, but I had the timeline wrong. I need your help to get these documents completed." His staff came together as a team, established a plan to complete the work, received a four-day extension from the district office, completed the work, and moved forward. This situation had never happened before. It was a mistake. The principal was brave enough to be honest, admit his mistake, and ask for help. He built trust with his staff at the same time. If he continued to make such errors, he would obviously not be building trust. But when the mistakes are few and far between, staff members are willing to pitch in to assist.

As I was facilitating a question-and-answer segment at a conference session, a superintendent asked me if a principal could be too vulnerable. My experience has shown me that's it very rare for a principal to be too vulnerable. I explained that if a principal makes mistakes frequently, apologizes often, and communicates unclearly with the school and teachers, then there is a problem with the principal's competence, not the principal's vulnerability. There is a distinct difference.

As you become more vulnerable and continue to build trust with your staff, you should be aware of two areas of caution: (1) predictive trust and (2) the fundamental attribution error (Lencioni, 2017). Let's begin with predictive trust. This type of trust occurs when you, as principal, unconsciously assume what other staff members will think or do in a particular situation. You, as leader, jump to conclusions about people's intent. Principals need to guard against predicting what staff members will think, say, or do. Just because they've worked in your school for several years does not mean you know what they believe about specific issues. I say this as a word of caution for new principals as they begin their leadership: know it's essential to get to know staff members so you can make your own decisions about them and not predict how they will behave because of what you've heard about them. Sliding into predictive trust at times is easy to do. If a team member of mine wasn't at our last meeting, I would find myself saying something like, "She won't care if we assign her to this task. She'll go along with anything we decide." Sometimes, I wouldn't even go back and discuss the new assignment with that team member. Or even worse, I would find myself thinking, "It doesn't matter what we do; he'll never be on board or positive about this initiative." I was predicting team members' thoughts and actions, and many times, my predictions were not accurate.

The second area of caution in building trust is the fundamental attribution error that can be placed on staff members. This stifles trust building, and leaders need to avoid it. The term *fundamental attribution error* can sound a bit confusing, but it's a simple concept. It's where you attribute other people's negative behaviors to their character (you make an *internal attribution*), but when *you* display a negative behavior, you attribute it to the environment (you make an *external attribution*; Lencioni, 2017). Here's an example of internal attribution: When a teacher makes a mistake, like arriving late to a meeting or not turning in required data, a leader might sometimes place a negative attribute on the individual. One might say things like, "She's lazy," or "I wish he'd be more committed to this project," or "I wish she'd get rid of her bad attitude about helping with this project." Comments like these are not about the action itself but about the person. These comments can be extremely hurtful to that particular person and also to staff members present when the comment is made. They leave staff feeling uncomfortable and wondering what might be said about them when they are not in the room.

If leaders trapped in that mindset make a similar mistake, they engage in external attribution and simply state the cause as an environmental reason. A reason like a sick child, missing data in a report, or a broken school printer means they couldn't complete their part of the work. But they avoid negative comments about their own character. Just be cautious. It's really easy to place these negative fundamental attributions on team members or yourself. You never want your colleagues wondering whether you will attribute negative behaviors to their character. When you do it as a leader, you damage the trust you are building with your team. When you allow others to do it, you allow the same damage.

As you build trust in your leadership, be vulnerable and use caution with predictive trust and fundamental attributions. Let's look at one more area to consider with trust building: reliability. If you want to continue building trust, you must be reliable. That is, do what you say and say what you do. Be reliable in your conversations with staff members. When staff members share information with you that should not be shared with others, demonstrate respect for confidentiality and never share that information. Build trust. Build relationships. And if staff members come to share information with you that you don't need to hear, as in gossip about others, demonstrate leadership by using answers like, "I'm not sure that's yours to share with me. I'll wait and see if they choose to tell me that information."

Being reliable is a huge trust builder. Brené Brown (2017) writes, "[Reliability] means staying aware of your competencies and limitations so you don't overpromise and are able to deliver on commitments and balance competing priorities" (p. 38). She uses the metaphor of a marble jar for thinking about being reliable and building trust. Every time you make a small gesture in support of your staff members, you put a marble in the jar. Every time you stay true to your word, you put a marble in the jar. Every time you follow through on your commitments, you put a marble in the jar. And conversely, every time you neglect to make a small gesture to support your staff members, you remove a marble from the jar. Every time you are not true to your word, you remove a marble from the jar. Every time you fail to follow through on your commitments, you remove a marble from the jar. You can build trust through this ongoing process of putting marbles in the jar. And you can just as easily lose trust by removing marbles through your actions. You can't really demand or force people to trust you. You must earn trust. And you earn it with consistent, intentional actions that put marbles in the jar. Leadership coach Thomas M. Van Soelen (2021), in his book about facilitating effective meetings, puts it like this: "Trust is an *outcome*, not a *behavior*" (p. 4).

I remember one occasion in my teaching career that exemplifies the importance of reliability and trust. I was getting ready for my evaluation session with my principal. He had scheduled the session for a Thursday morning and said he would come to my classroom. I was a bit nervous, but also very excited. I couldn't wait to share some student data, a few student writing pieces, and the new short story unit I had written.

He never showed up. I never received a call or an email. After school, I stopped by his secretary's office to make certain I had the right date. She said it was the correct date, but he had been very busy all day and couldn't get to me. A few days later, I received an email with a new date for our evaluation session. Once again, he didn't show. I didn't even bother checking on it this time. The next week, my evaluation form—complete with checkmarks and scores—was waiting for me in my teacher mailbox. The marks were all good. But I was not. My principal had not been reliable. I had lost trust in him. I felt he didn't think our time together was a priority for him. He had taken several marbles out of the jar and had absolutely no idea. His leadership could have built substantial trust with me, just by showing up. It reminds me of this quote by leadership authority John Maxwell (2010): "When you make a commitment, you create hope. When you keep a commitment, you create trust" (p. 236). Make a commitment to working hard as a leader who continually builds deeper and deeper trust with your staff.

Have Difficult Conversations

Another way to build relationships with your staff is one you might not naturally think of in a positive light. It's the ability to have difficult conversations with your staff members. You might think this ability doesn't fit in this chapter and is better suited for chapter 8 (page 131), where we'll discuss holding people accountable. But I have intentionally placed it here because of its capacity to build trust with your staff. You build trust with people when you're willing to have real dialogue with them about difficult situations. The results are twofold: not only do you build trust with the staff member you're talking to, but you also build trust with other teachers and staff members throughout the school. They understand that when issues need to be discussed with staff members who are not doing what's required, you'll have those conversations. They build trust in your leadership. Difficult conversations seem to have a far-reaching effect when it comes to building trust.

The semester principal playbook goals may provide an area where you need to have a difficult conversation. These goals should be challenging and involve hard work. You want no room for "gotcha!" in your school where you try to catch staff members doing something wrong. Instead, you have conversations with your staff to set clear expectations for what needs to be done, support teachers in that work, and handle poor performance when necessary. There is no way around the fact that difficult conversations with teachers who are underperforming must occur. The work is complex, teachers will struggle at times, and you must be ready to give the support and clarity they need. These conversations require brave leadership.

If you do not confront poor instruction, you risk the onset of mediocrity that could permeate the school environment. In addition, you risk the possibility of your best teachers seeing that other teachers can get by with mediocre instruction and no evidence of student learning in their classrooms. The result? Your best teachers can become discouraged and, potentially, less motivated to improve and grow. They can lose trust in their leader. And many will decide to leave the school. Teachers and staff members must know that the small things won't slide and that all staff members will be held to high expectations. They deserve to trust that difficult conversations will be part of your leadership.

Hanig and Senge (2015) have a model for difficult conversations, illustrated in figure 6.1 (page 110), that has made such a difference for me by providing structure to facilitate dialogue. In using this model, you begin the conversation at the bottom-left quartile, with polite conversation. Quickly, you move to the lower-right quartile, where you approach the disagreement. When things become uncomfortable in the disagreement quartile, you have three choices of action: (1) return to politeness; (2) react, break down, freak out; or (3) move upward into inquiry. Instead of easily slipping back into polite conversation, you must practice leading the conversation up into the inquiry quartile. This is where we, as leaders, ask questions to help better understand the situation—for example, "Help me understand; tell me more," "Why do you see things that way?" or "How do you think we can move forward from here and fix things?" It's critical to remain open to questions the other participant is asking of you and intentionally hear whatever questions that person may have. Only after both participants have shared these questions and thoughts can the conversation move into the upper-left quartile, where real dialogue can take place and solutions can be found. You can't operate a school by just skimming over the surface of difficult topics and situations. You must be willing to have these difficult conversations and skilled at having them. They are a necessary part of building relationships and trust with your staff.

Let's work our way through the real dialogue model by using a personal example. In my second year as principal, a teacher came to school late several times one quarter. Two other teachers on her department team reported her tardiness to me. They complained that she wasn't there for her hallway and restroom supervision duties in the morning and they were trying to cover her assignments. They also noted she hadn't been there for the beginning of several English department meetings. Since she served as the English department teacher

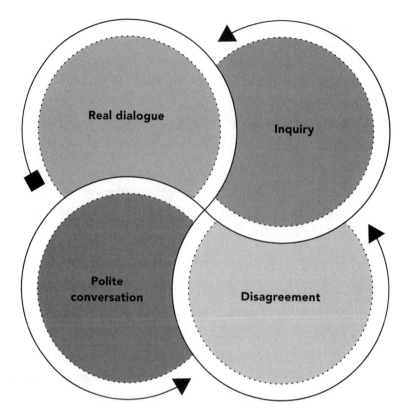

Source: Adapted from Hanig & Senge, 2015.

Figure 6.1: Real dialogue model.

leader, this was definitely an issue. The English teachers went ahead and started those meetings without her. When these teachers approached me, the first thought in my mind was, "Well, have you all said anything to her?" But I had to stop myself. I knew I couldn't ask them that. How could I ask them to hold her accountable when I hadn't done so myself?

I needed to gather some data, which I did over the following two weeks. This particular teacher came in late, sometimes only two to three minutes, two times in eight days. Now I had some data to use in our conversation. I didn't need to use information reported by other staff members. I could speak with her about what I had observed myself.

After school, I went down to her room and began with polite conversation, asking about her children. Then I moved into the bottom-right quartile and let her know that I had observed her coming in tardy two times in the last eight days. I shared detailed information: specific days, specific arrival times, and so on. She immediately began to share all the reasons for her lateness. I was aware she had several things going on in her personal life, but she shared even more details. She became emotional and defensive. I listened. When she was finished, it would have been so easy for me to say, "Well, I know there's a lot on your plate right now, so try to do better." But I knew that wasn't real dialogue. Even with her emotional response and defensiveness, I knew I had to keep the conversation going. With deliberateness, I moved the conversation up into the inquiry quartile and began asking questions.

Problem presented by others
Gather data for yourself observations
Start with polite conversation
→ share your observation specifics
more to inquiry ask questions, possible solutions
Support and help

Possible reactions
defensiveness, excuses,
emotional responses →

"Can you help me understand if there's something I can do to help you get here on time? You know it doesn't matter how late you work each evening, right? I'm required to have you here on time. We need you here. It's beginning to affect your team. The English department needs your leadership. What can I do to help?" We discussed options like giving the teacher leader position to another English teacher for the year or having other teachers volunteer for her night duties. If we needed to take some things off her plate, I wanted her to know we could certainly do that.

We then moved into the final quartile of real dialogue, where she shared a few things that might help her. But more importantly, she knew what she needed to do. I made it very clear: the next tardy would require written documentation in her file. I certainly hoped it never got to that point, but I needed to be very clear. In the end, she was tardy once again several months later, and I documented it, had her sign the form, and placed it in her file. But after that, I never had to address her tardiness again. Her team members addressed her tardiness the only other time it occurred that year. They handled it. They trusted me for assistance if needed, but they chose to handle that incident. She wasn't tardy again that school year, and I removed the form from her file. We moved on.

Another situation in which I needed to have a difficult conversation and use the real dialogue model occurred in a special education conference meeting regarding one student. Seven staff members, the student's mother, and I were seated around the conference table. Lauren, the school psychologist, had completed the special education psychological testing and shared the results with the group, taking extra measures to communicate effectively with the parent. The teachers began sharing their concerns about this student with the mother. She was trying to take in all this information, but I could tell she didn't truly understand all our education jargon and she was too afraid to ask for clarification. Being outnumbered like that is already intimidating for a parent. One of the teachers made a sarcastic comment to the mother, saying, "Well, if I took as much interest in my child as you do in yours, I wouldn't understand all of this either." It was a mean comment. It was hurtful. It was disrespectful. I was embarrassed. Silence took over the room. Lauren and a few of the teachers looked down at their notes. A few teachers looked straight at me. I quietly asked the teacher if he would go to my office and get some paperwork for me. He left the conference room.

A few minutes later, I stepped outside the conference room and waited for him to return. When he walked up to hand me the documents, I explained that his comment was disrespectful and there was no place for hurtful words or sarcasm at our school. I said, "Thanks for the paperwork. There's no reason for you to rejoin the meeting. I'm concerned and disappointed in your comments to this mother, and we'll discuss things further tomorrow." I took the paperwork, returned to the conference room, and shut the door.

This wasn't the first time this teacher exhibited such behavior, and I should have addressed his comments in a previous situation. But this time, I knew my leadership required that I step up, handle the situation, and build trust with the others in the conference.

The next day at school, I had the conversation I should have had several months earlier. I began working through the real dialogue model in my head. Polite conversation was quick because we were both aware that we were there to handle a disagreement. It was tough. He became emotional and defensive as he tried to convince me that he was just joking with the parent. I held my ground. I knew I had to make my expectation clear: as long as I was principal and leading our school, hurtful, disrespectful comments were not acceptable.

We didn't spend much time in the inquiry quartile. I simply asked him to share with me how he thought his words would not be hurtful and condescending to the parent. He didn't really have an answer, so we moved on. In the real dialogue quadrant, I shared with him that every time I witnessed or was made aware of him saying something hurtful or condescending, I would come address it with him. I mentioned the situation where I had heard him say something to a student in the cafeteria that didn't feel good to me either. It was my mistake for not bringing that to his attention back when it happened. I made my concerns clear; I made my expectations clear. He knew that I expected him to improve his interactions with our students, staff members, and parents. Condescending comments and sarcastic, hurtful remarks were not acceptable.

It was a very difficult conversation. I was a bit shaky when it was over. I was not surprised when the teacher did not thank me, of course. But I was taken aback when I received thank-yous from three teachers who had participated in the conference with us. One teacher sent an email, and two others placed handwritten cards on my desk. The notes thanked me for addressing his comments and explained that he had been saying such things since several years before I had even arrived at the school. The notes shared that knowing their leader addressed those comments felt good and gave them the courage to do so themselves if such comments continued.

I felt good about those thank-you notes. But I also felt disappointed—in myself. I should have addressed the issue months earlier. It became clear to me that my lack of leadership in having these difficult conversations when needed was affecting other members of the staff. It took me too long to find the courage to have those conversations. But once I did, I was empowered by the trust it built with my staff who appreciated the effort of making our school into the place of excellence it could be, and of making our shared vision a reality. The outcome of that particular conversation seemed to be a good one. Throughout my remaining six years as principal, I only had one other conversation with that teacher about a comment he sarcastically made to a student. No other staff members or parents ever reported anything else. There were two possibilities: (1) maybe he had changed his behavior and wasn't making such comments any longer, or (2) maybe other staff members were addressing it themselves if they heard something that needed to be brought to his attention—or maybe a little of both.

These two examples of using the real dialogue model to lead difficult conversations—one about tardiness, one about respectful interaction with others—actually relate to a system I developed in my first year as a principal. I introduced what I called my top-ten expectations for teachers as a component of every opening day with staff (see figure 6.2). I was looking for a way to share basic expectations with staff. It was only fair that they had a clear understanding of what their leader expected. These expectations were very basic things that should never require discussion during the year. A few examples would include arriving at school on time and performing one's responsibilities, always having a rigorous plan ready for

---

Top-Ten Expectations

1. Know your essential curriculum better than I do! Be ready to have discussions about students and their learning in your classroom.

2. Review your quarterly CFA data, and be ready to discuss specific concerns and solutions for making our instruction better.

3. Be aware that I consider your classroom sacred territory, and I will guard against unnecessary interruptions.

4. Be respectful and professional always.

5. Come to me when I make mistakes.

6. Speak positively about our school in public and on social media platforms.

7. Work hard—each day, every period.

8. Acknowledge, but don't enable, our students.

9. Grow! Find ways to learn more and get even better.

10. Be brilliant at the following basics.

    • Know our faculty handbook.

    • Be on time.

    • Attend all department or grade-level meetings, collaborations, and faculty meetings.

    • Be at your door (or assigned area) ready to go at 8:50 a.m.

    • Sit with your students at assemblies.

    • Monitor our hallways and restrooms during each passing period.

    • Meet deadline requests.

    • Be on time to pick up your students from lunch.

    • Return parent phone calls and emails promptly.

    • Have your substitute handbook completed and ready to go.

Figure 6.2: Example top-ten expectations.

*Reproduce
Make a poster
Post in office,
Near mailboxes, teacher
lounge*

a substitute, and following the non-negotiables and commitments on the pacing guides. I also included things like speaking positively about the school when in public and on social media, treating each student with respect, and understanding that I considered the classroom a sacred place for learning and growing, so teachers should use each minute wisely.

As I said, you shouldn't need to have discussions with teachers about any of these basic expectations. But every single year, I found it necessary. The top-ten expectations became a useful tool for me to use when having difficult conversations. I presented the top-ten expectations only once each year: on opening day with teachers. After that, I used the real dialogue model with individual staff members in individual situations where one of the expectations needed addressing. Consider developing your own top-ten expectations to use on your opening day.

When you set clear expectations for your staff and address those expectations when broken, you create more and more trust, building a healthy school environment. Your interactions will

People prefer uncomfortable truth over comfortable lies.

SIVE CHS AD Interim
I was told comfortable lies

demonstrate honest, meaningful feedback. You talk straight and let people know where you stand. You call things as they are and don't leave false impressions for people to think things are better than they actually are. You know your staff and listen to their differing points of view without assuming you always know what's best. You build relationships through difficult conversations. In my leadership, I have grown to believe that people sincerely prefer the uncomfortable truth over the comfortable lies. Author and activist Glennon Doyle (2020) writes, "Every truth is a kindness, even if it makes others uncomfortable. Every untruth is an unkindness, even if it makes others comfortable" (p. 112).

Ensure Your People Find Meaning in Their Work

Poster

As you continually work on building relationships, it just makes sense to concentrate your efforts on knowing each of your staff. You may remember that in chapter 4 (page 65), we discussed the importance of every staff member's time. We discussed how effective principals should ensure they know their noncertified staff members and their families; should ensure the staff members' roles at the school are defined, clear, and meaningful; and should ensure the staff members have goals that can be measured each semester. Maybe it goes without saying, but I want to mention it here as we discuss building relationships: you, as leader, must make absolutely certain that every single adult working in your school feels seen, heard, and known. Your actions must show your staff members that you think each of them is worthwhile as you consistently notice and comment on things they do well. This is especially true for educators working in a virtual environment. You must work hard to assist all your staff members to find their meaning in your school's work and nourish their roles. They should each have a clear understanding of their significance in the school, and a way to measure their work. Create an environment where people want to work and grow.

As human beings, your staff members want their work to be meaningful, so helping each of them find meaning in their work is among your responsibilities. Let's think about what meaningful work really looks like. Researchers Catherine Bailey and Adrian Madden (2016) study the factors that create—or destroy—a sense of meaning in the workplace. Meaningful work is that in which your staff members can have a sense of pride and in which they can feel they are reaching their potential. Meaningful work involves making a difference for other individuals or groups. And it can also be really hard work, even uncomfortable at times, but every bit worth the effort when others see that the results make a difference (Bailey & Madden, 2016).

How can you help build a sense of meaningful work for your staff? By being a leader who provides a clear understanding of the purpose and vision of your school and then demonstrates how each job or role fits within that purpose and makes a difference. You also must be a leader who takes the time to have thoughtful, intentional one-on-one dialogues about each person's completed work and acknowledge the specific things each person has accomplished. When things aren't going well, you show that you know your people and care about them. When your teachers aren't making progress and seem to be struggling, you show that you care about them as human beings. You make certain they're OK, and then you move on to discuss their outcomes.

Are there ways you can cause the work to be meaningless? In their research, Bailey and Madden (2016) have found that "meaningfulness is largely something that individuals must find for themselves in their work, but meaninglessness is something that organizations and leaders can actively cause" (p. 58). Poor leadership can destroy your staff's ability to find meaning. Meaninglessness comes from taking employees for granted and not recognizing hard work. It's not saying, "Thank you," when they perform extra duties. It's allowing them to feel unrecognized, unacknowledged, and underappreciated. It's giving them pointless, meaningless tasks to do.

Building relationships is a day-to-day experience. Each decision you make, each comment you speak, and each action you take as a leader either builds or negates the relationships you are trying to develop. Each action can be meaningful or meaningless. This work of consistently building relationships is certainly not easy. It takes intentionality to avoid blaming the issues in your school on external factors all the time. It's easy to place blame elsewhere, and many principals do exactly that. Instead of looking at their own leadership and ways to improve their school from within, these principals simply blame outside factors. They get angry, defensive, and negative about things being done to their school—state or provincial initiatives and testing are just two examples. Highly effective principals push through the negativity and excuses. Choose to develop yourself, to develop meaningful relationships with your staff, and to assist your staff in finding meaning in their work.

Building Trust Takes Heart

If you are going to build trust within yourself and within your staff relationships, you must be a brave leader. That takes courage. Just as I discussed in the introduction of this book, it demands leading and speaking with your whole heart. It most certainly takes heart and spirit to lead a school. It requires being vulnerable. It requires being reliable. It requires hard, uncomfortable conversations. It requires clear expectations. It requires getting to know your staff and what's going on in their lives. It requires protecting them from too many initiatives. It requires protecting them from negative behaviors in the school. And it requires self-awareness and a willingness to address your own insecurities to become the courageous leader you strive to be.

Simply put, building relationships may be the most important work you can do. Work hard to earn the trust of your people. Make certain they each feel heard, valued, known, and empowered by their trusted leader.

To reflect on building relationships and begin work on your next steps, see the reproducible tools on pages 116–118.

Self-Rating Scale for Trust-Building Measures

As you consistently work on building relationships in your school, take some time to reflect on your work in building trust with your staff members, students, and school families. Use the following template to self-rate your current level of implementation for each area.

Trust-Building Measures	Consistent Implementation	Approaching Consistent Implementation	Average Implementation	Sporadic Implementation	Marginal or No Implementation
Be vulnerable.					
Avoid using predictive trust.					
Avoid using the fundamental attribution error.					
Be reliable.					

Real Dialogue Practice Sheet

Think about the most recent difficult conversation you have had with a staff member. Reflect on the good things that came from the conversation and anything that you could have improved. Now think of a difficult conversation you know you need to have in the near future. Use the following template to help you prepare for that conversation. Jot down a few notes for each quadrant to help you get ready for this real dialogue.

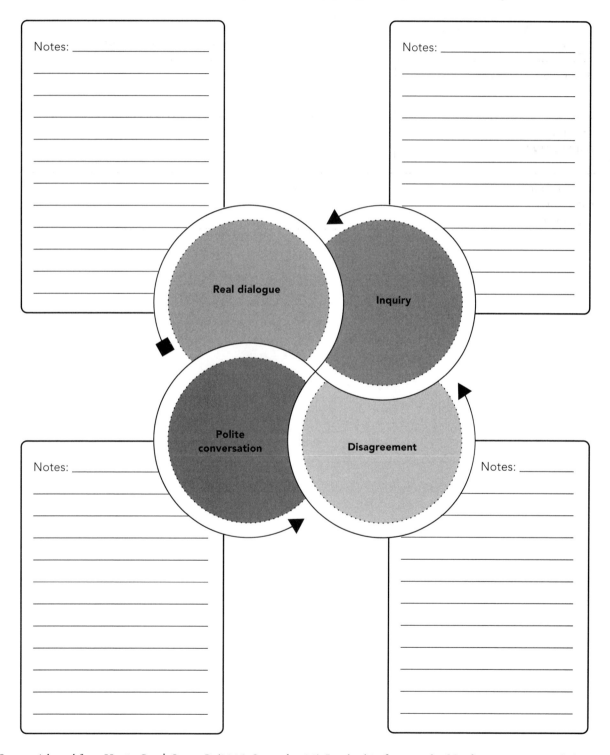

Notes: _____

Notes: _____

Notes: _____

Notes: _____

Source: Adapted from Hanig, R., & Senge, P. (2015, September 29). Leadership frameworks [Conference presentation]. Society for Organizational Learning workshop, Ashland, MA.

Top-Ten Expectations Template

Review the example top-ten expectations in figure 6.2 (page 113).

Now take a few minutes to begin creating your own top-ten expectations. Jot down your ideas and thoughts in the following template. Make it your own. If you want only five or six expectations, that works. Just personalize the things you want to clarify with staff.

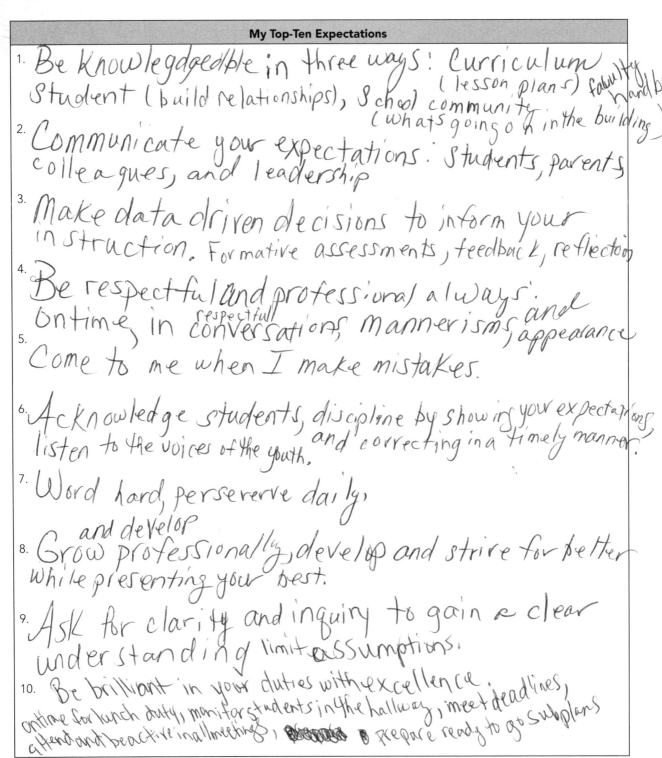

My Top-Ten Expectations

1. Be knowlegdeable in three ways: Curriculum (lesson plans) faculty handbook Student (build relationships), School community (whats going on in the building)

2. Communicate your expectations: Students, parents, colleagues, and leadership

3. Make data driven decisions to inform your instruction. Formative assessments, feedback, reflection

4. Be respectful and professional always: Ontime, in respectful conversations, mannerisms, and appearance

5. Come to me when I make mistakes.

6. Acknowledge students, discipline by showing your expectations, listen to the voices of the youth. and correcting in a timely manner.

7. Word hard, persererve daily, and develop

8. Grow professionally, develop and strive for better while presenting your best.

9. Ask for clarity and inquiry to gain a clear understanding limit assumptions.

10. Be brilliant in your duties with excellence. ontime for lunch duty, monifor students in the hallway, meet deadlines, attend and be active in all meetings, prepare ready to go subplans

CHAPTER 7

Reframe Conflict

A dear friend, and fellow educator, asked me right after we both retired, "Rhonda, what was the one lesson that took you the longest to learn as a principal?" I had to think long and hard about my answer, and then I replied, "It took me too long to understand that conflict goes with leadership. It took me too long to quit striving toward the day when there would be no conflict. It took me too long to realize that conflict can be a good thing!" That's exactly why this chapter is in this book. I don't want it to take you as long as it took me to understand conflict and reframe your thinking with a new perspective.

As you start to be more intentional in strengthening your skill of building relationships, especially with a strong foundation of trust, it becomes much easier to address conflicts when they arise in your school. These conflicts come in all shapes and sizes—small issues and huge issues, issues between two people and issues involving groups. But one thing is for certain: effective principals frame their conflicts with a positive perspective. They face them and work diligently to address them in positive, meaningful ways. They reframe their thinking and begin to see conflict as an opportunity, as fuel to provide forward momentum. Leaders have a choice to make when it comes to conflict. They can do one of three things: (1) avoid it, (2) attack it, or (3) address it (Feirsen & Weitzman, 2021). Let's get to work addressing it!

In this chapter, we will look at four ideas for you to consider when reframing conflict: (1) accept that conflict will be part of your leadership, (2) mine for conflict, (3) acknowledge others who address conflict, and (4) understand that conflict requires tough decisions. Let's get going.

Accept That Conflict Will Be Part of Your Leadership

There's no other way to say it: just accept that conflict will always be part of your leadership—period. When you incorporate the five essential leadership actions from part 1 (page 9) into the daily work of your school, you require much from your staff. Those actions will lead to some staff members getting upset. Conflict will definitely become a reality for you. You might think you've created a solid team until it gets down to doing the really difficult work of changing instruction and challenging each other to dig deeper for more engaging ways of teaching.

Effective principals don't try to avoid conflict. Having a grounded understanding that conflict can be healthy and productive is a must. This was hard for me to accept in my first years as principal. I had to quit working toward that utopia where everyone would be happy with me. I had to quit working for that day when there would be no teacher concerns, no district office disagreements, no parent misunderstandings, no student behavior issues, and no ball-game brawls. That day never comes. And it took me too many years to fully understand and appreciate the positive aspects of conflict. I had to reframe my thinking from dreaming of the day when there would be no conflicts to dreaming about the opportunities that conflict could bring.

As the leader, you must learn to be comfortable when things are uncomfortable—such a simple statement to make, such a difficult thing to do. Tolerating mediocre and poor performance is one of the worst things you can do. But it sure is easy to let this performance just go unnoticed. Learning to address these essential things with staff members, to actively listen, to organize a plan, and to sit in silence is so hard to do—especially sitting in silence while waiting for someone to respond! But the more I addressed the conflicts, learned to develop solutions, and nudged people forward, the more comfortable I became with addressing conflict.

Addressing conflict also forced me to confront some shortcomings in my own leadership and get past my need to always be right, always be liked, and always be in control. I had to begin viewing conflict as an opportunity. I had to believe in the positive results that conflict could bring. Avoiding people, avoiding situations, avoiding meetings, and avoiding uncomfortable evaluations were not options any longer. I accepted the uneasiness, stepped into the conflict, and came out better on the other side.

Mine for Conflict

Why in the world would you go looking for conflict if you don't see any? Because this lack of conflict—what I call *artificial harmony*—usually means you or your team members might not be sharing honest thoughts and opinions. You have a responsibility to look for these honest feelings. It's up to you to state the obvious areas of concern and begin the dialogue. Remember that leaders must be the people who extract the buried disagreements and shed some light on the issues (Lencioni, 2002).

Let's be clear. You can't make avoiding conflict a top priority. You can't act like it's not there. My experience has shown me that when principals report everything is going well and there are no concerns, that's simply not the case. Those same principals have not been in classrooms to see if curricular commitments are actually embedded. They have not attended a collaboration meeting to see what actually happens. They have not joined an intervention class to see if the reteaching and targeted assistance are really taking place. It's much easier to assume things are happening and to believe there are no issues, no concerns, and no need to address anything. It's definitely easier, but it's not leadership.

I like the analogy of viewing conflict as a swimming pool. Far too many times, principals keep the discussion at an artificial harmony level—the shallow end of the pool. Everybody feels safe, so they tend to simply splash around there; no meaningful conversations occur,

[Handwritten margin notes:]
Learn to be comfortable when things are uncomfortable. Sit in silence wait patiently on a response.

You are not always right, be liked, and in control. View conflict as an opportunity. Conflict can bring positive results.

Know for yourself. This is not leadership

Lack of conflict is artificial harmony

and no meaningful changes in behavior take place. It might feel easier to stay in the shallow end because it's frightening to swim out to the deepest water, where mean-spirited arguments can arise. But a true leader encourages people to swim out to the deep end, where teams can begin to discuss the difficult issues, such as why students are not achieving on certain concepts, and work together to solve those issues. You can do this when you've built relationships with your staff. That's using conflict in a constructive way. Good things can happen—such as teachers admitting they need help with an instructional piece and developing new strategies for difficult concepts—when you get staff members to be open and discuss the difficult issues. If the conversation does become too heated, with harsh words or negative feelings, then *lead*. Take control of the conversation, and lead your team back to a healthy place of dialogue.

It happened at Scribner during a meeting with our school's science department when the seven people in attendance—four science teachers, two English teachers, and I—were discussing a requirement of a quarterly argumentative writing piece. Conflict erupted. The English teachers were trying to assist the science teachers in a structured process for writing an argumentative piece. Things were going pretty well until one science teacher stood up, threw his pen on the table, and shouted that there was no way he had time to do this writing stuff in his science class. This was a first-year teacher, and he was feeling the pressure of teaching the science core indicators and finding ways for all his students to reach proficiency on his assessments. We were trying to establish a way to use argumentative writing within one of the science experiment write-ups. This would not have been an addition to his teaching—he was already doing writing pieces—just a way to add in the argumentative elements. But at that moment, it just felt like too much change. He fired off a few inappropriate phrases and stomped out of the classroom. I let the silence reign for a few moments. Then I spoke up for him and explained to the teachers in the room that he must be feeling overwhelmed as a new teacher. While I was speaking, he came back in the room, apologized for his actions and words, and then asked if we could start again. He commented that he felt he wasn't a good writer himself, so he was asking for as much guidance as he could get. I had given him time to cool off for a few minutes, and then he was ready for more discussion. We all learned from the experience. He chose to be vulnerable and learned we were going to support him through the writing piece each step of the way. I learned to give more encouragement for all the work he'd been doing with our science units. The English teachers learned that more frequent check-ins with them would be invaluable for him in the upcoming semester.

Curricular expectations were high. Our English department was asking teachers to do their part in helping students become better writers—in all subjects. Using the analogy of the swimming pool, we got down toward the deep end in that science meeting because we were pushing against the science teachers' comfort zone. But it was all right. You can lead through this type of conflict. Get things settled back down, take a break, and then come back together to find solutions. Conflicts are opportunities for growth. Our English department had only requested one argumentative piece from the science teachers for the year, but the science team decided to incorporate a piece into several more of their units. Our science teachers grew in their understanding of writing; our English teachers grew as coaches of the writing process; and our students became better writers. If you don't have any conflicts in your school, you better look harder to find some.

Acknowledge Others Who Address Conflict

Your own handling of conflict is obviously a key aspect of leadership, but equally important is your acknowledgment when a staff member is brave enough to bring up an area of conflict. If this happens during a meeting, address the fact that a staff member was courageous enough to go there (whatever the difficult issue is) for the betterment of the school. Thank the staff member for caring enough to do that. You could say something like, "It's a really tough topic, but thank you for having the courage to bring it up today. We're beginning to come to some possible solutions now because you had the courage to speak up." No one should leave the meeting wondering whether you're upset because a staff member brought up the conflict.

Acknowledging staff members who bring up a difficult topic reminds me of a task I did in my first year as principal. The district office had asked all principals to review their school's vision, mission, and belief statements. *Belief statements* are declarative sentences that state what your staff values. A few examples would be *Our teachers build relationships that engage students in learning* or *Our teachers are dedicated, enthusiastic, lifelong learners.* Most principals just checked with a few staff members in their schools to make certain they had the most recent copies of the documents and sent them right on to the district office. Mission accomplished. But as a new principal, I knew I didn't like the wordiness of our school's statements and was hoping the staff could just revise them a bit and make them more succinct. I had decided to use an introductory activity in our full faculty meeting and then told the staff that I would be spending a full day meeting with teachers during their planning periods so we could discuss the current vision, mission, and belief statements and I could get verbal feedback and suggested revisions.

On the day I was meeting with staff, first and second periods went just as I had expected. Staff members read the documents and suggested a few innocent revisions, like changing *some* to *few*. Easy discussions. Quick changes. No real dialogue. And then I hit third period with a mix of social studies and physical education teachers. I handed out the district template with the vision, mission, and belief statements and began reviewing each one. When a social studies teacher said, "I think this belief statement sums us up pretty well: *we do whatever it takes for our students to achieve,*" most people in the room agreed and wanted to include it as one of our key behaviors as a staff. Things were rolling right along. After several minutes of people sharing all kinds of examples about how great we were and what teachers were doing to help students, one physical education and health teacher spoke up and had the guts to say:

> I don't think that's really true. I don't think all of us really do whatever it takes for kids to learn. Some of us just want to keep doing what we've always done and don't want to really look at new ways to help our students learn better. That's a lot of work. I just don't agree that we do whatever it takes. And while I'm at it, I don't agree with the belief statement that *Our school is a warm and inviting*

community for our parents. I don't think we are warm to our parents sometimes. I hear some of us making negative comments about our parents daily,
and we sure don't want to have conferences with them when they reach out to
us. That's what I honestly think.

The room got quiet. I allowed the silence to hang heavy on all of us for a few minutes.
No one said another word. Some people thought I might be upset about the teacher's comment. I knew I needed to acknowledge this teacher's bravery for speaking up.

"I agree with you, Paul," I responded. I allowed that to sink in with everyone for a couple
of minutes and then continued, "Yes, I agree with you. And I thank you for being honest
and forcing us to take a deeper look at ourselves, even when we don't like everything we see."

The conversation turned at that point, and it really surprised me. Most everyone opened
up to say they understood what Paul was saying. Although some staff were doing whatever it took for our students to make progress, it was not a consistent action among our
leadership team members, much less across the school. And we could certainly do more to
become a warm and inviting place for our parents. We decided to make these aspirational
goals for our behaviors instead of claiming them as being embedded already. We had every
intent to move forward, but we knew we weren't there yet.

The rest of the planning period visits that afternoon went well. Word traveled quickly that
Paul had shared his honest opinions. But, just as importantly, word also spread that Paul's
thoughts and comments were accepted well by me and his colleagues.

If conflict is going to become a good and worthy thing to move your school forward, you
must create a safe place for it. Staff members should be able to discuss any topic with you.
Some principals, without being aware of it, create undiscussables in their schools. *Undiscussables*
are items or topics that staff members learn not to bring up around their principal.

As I think back over my years as a teacher, counselor, and assistant principal, in which
I worked with several principals, an undiscussable comes to mind from the leadership in
one school. In my teaching years, my fellow teachers and I knew to never ask our principal
about decreasing the minutes used for passing time between periods. We had six minutes
and wanted to move it to four. Our facility wasn't very large, and students could easily
make it to their lockers and on to their classes. But our principal never wanted to discuss
this. He once explained that changing the bell system would take an unnecessary amount
of work and he wasn't willing to do that. Things were working just fine, and he could not
understand why we wanted a couple more minutes of instruction. Even though we tried
to explain that gaining five minutes each day throughout the school year would give us an
additional two or three days of instruction, he didn't care. He wasn't changing the clocks.
When he got extremely upset at our last request, we knew we would never bring it up again.
It had just become an undiscussable.

Friends of mine who are principals have shared with me several examples of undiscussables
from their experiences. Some of these will sound outright silly, but these are real examples:
Never ask for a student's schedule to be changed if it's after the principal's deadline; that is
undiscussable. Don't bring up any ideas to make the cafeteria run more efficiently; that is

undiscussable. Don't ask if the superintendent's administrative meeting could be held any day but Friday; that is undiscussable. Don't ask to review suspension data and student arrest data by ethnicity; that is undiscussable. Most of you experienced undiscussables when you served as classroom teachers. Make certain you're not creating any undiscussables in the schools you lead.

Understand That Conflict Requires Tough Decisions

When you have difficult decisions to make, you can count on conflict coming along for the ride. Most times, you can make these tough decisions with your leadership team. As I worked hard on trying to be reflective and make the best decisions possible, I read about a process with four decision-making steps (Balch & Brower, 2005) that helped me organize and plan for big decisions.

This decision-making process has four steps that can help you organize and plan for a decision. First, always discuss why the decision has to be made in the first place. Second, facilitate numerous discussions on the item. I like to facilitate these discussions in multiple small groups instead of as an entire staff. Third, after meeting in small groups, lead a clarification meeting with the entire staff, explaining what you've learned from everyone and what solutions have become available. Finally, after much reflection, share the final decision that will be made in the best interests of the entire school. This decision-making process (Balch & Brower, 2005) is a way for you to come to a final decision for the health of the entire organization. Here's a recap of the decision-making steps.

1. Discuss why the decision has to be made in the first place.

2. Conduct small-group meetings to listen and hear as much input as possible.

3. Lead a clarification session for all staff.

4. Share the final decision.

I have a gut-wrenching example of having to make a really tough decision. Because of financial issues, our district office gave me the following directive: Scribner Middle School needed to eliminate three full-time teaching positions. This reduction could include retirements, with the understanding that those positions would not be replaced. If possible, those teachers losing their current positions would be moved into open positions at another school, but no one could promise that. So the journey began. Who should be let go? Staff members had differing opinions, and I was in the midst of some major conflict.

My first step was to begin with the why. In a full faculty meeting, I shared as much information as I could about the school district's financial situation and why the school was being asked to let go of three full-time teaching positions. I made certain to share all the other reductions the district had made before finding it necessary to have a reduction in staff. The faculty presented several questions to consider, including, Was it possible to reduce our academic core teachers and still provide acceleration time (also called *remediation* or *intervention*) for struggling learners and enrichment time for students ready for more? and How could we make certain that all students were receiving electives? We really wanted to keep all our academic core and elective teachers, but it was no longer possible.

My next step was to organize staff to meet in small groups to share lots of deep discussion, other possibilities, and everyone's thoughts. Each period, I met with a group of seven to eleven staff members on their planning time. Throughout the conversations, new options came to the surface. A key thing to remember for these meetings, as in all your school's meetings, is that you must be willing to say things that need to be said. You must urge your staff members not to go behind people's backs, not to wait until after the meeting to say what they think. It's messy. It's hard. And often, it's uncomfortable. But you actually want to experience some pain in your meetings so that you protect your school from much more pain later.

Ultimately, staff made it clear in the small-group sessions that we should try to keep all academic core teachers in order to provide core curriculum with acceleration time for our struggling students. That meant the three lost positions would come from our elective courses. We would still be able to offer most, but not all, students two electives. As I look back, I'm not thoroughly convinced it was the best option. But at the time, we were trying to build and sustain a solid academic core focused on student learning, and we had numerous students not achieving at grade level.

Before I even held the clarification session with the entire staff to inform them of all the options from the small-group sessions, one physical education teacher came to me in private to say he was going to retire. He did not want the staff to know until school was out for the summer. He had seriously been thinking about it for two years, and the small-group conversation that day led him to be secure in his decision to move forward with his retirement. He was an elective teacher.

Another teacher received word that she would be moving over the summer. She was a reading intervention teacher, and we wouldn't be able to replace her. Now we were down to losing one more teacher from our elective departments who had the least tenure. I didn't agree with our district's thinking at the time (and they don't do this any longer) of "last teacher in, first teacher out." Our most recent hire was making a significant difference for students by developing engaging units of study in her classroom. I did not want to lose her. I made several attempts to move a different teacher to another school, but ultimately, it was not my choice. I knew I had to make the best of the situation and since the teacher would be moving to teach at one of our high schools, I tried to support her every step of the way. Our remaining physical education teachers absorbed the loss of our retired physical education teacher and made things work effectively. We found new options for getting our struggling readers the help they needed by training our special education teachers and some of our instructional assistants in reading strategies with guided groups. And all of our remaining elective teachers absorbed the students of the teacher who was placed at the high school. Those elective teachers pulled together as a team and developed a new elective rotation schedule for students.

The final two steps of the decision-making process were addressed in our next faculty meeting. I made certain to clarify all the options from our small-group meetings and then shared the final decision. From that entire process, the small-group conversations stand out. People really gave their full attention to the conversation and spoke up with their thoughts and ideas. There were not many concerns from the physical education staff when they knew their class sizes would increase. They understood why and made the higher class loads work. The special education teachers came to me to ask what they could do for the loss of the reading teacher. And that motivated me to make certain I held our remaining elective teachers accountable for effective instruction in their classrooms, just as the teacher who was moved from our school had provided. We had lost one of our most effective teachers, but we were all going to get better because of it.

You Can Practice Addressing Conflict

I've discussed accepting that conflict will be part of your leadership. I've talked about mining for conflict, acknowledging others who address conflict, and making really tough decisions. Here are a few other suggestions of things you might want to consider while addressing conflict.

- Promote calm, not drama. Adult drama can be really difficult.

- Be respectful, not condescending.

- Hear others' voices, not just your own.

- Stick to the issue at hand without wandering off to other topics.

- Use accurate sources without making sweeping statements like, "Everyone thinks this, not just me."

- Own the responsibility of doing the work and making the decisions without placing blame.

Conflict is a really difficult part of leadership. Stop avoiding it and reframe your thinking. Start addressing it. Build your conflict skills each and every time you're willing to address an issue. Build your conflict skills each and every time you're willing to go find issues when there appear to be none. Build your conflict skills when you don't react to negative, toxic energy. Instead, respond with a clear perspective of addressing conflict and finding opportunities for your school and staff to grow.

To reflect on reframing conflict and begin work on your next steps, see the reproducible tools on pages 127–129.

Writing Prompts for Developing Your Conflict-Framing Skills

Review each of the four ideas to consider when reframing conflict. Then in the space provided, write down a few sentences in response to each writing prompt.

Idea 1: Accept that conflict will be part of your leadership.

Writing prompt: Each time a conflict arises over the next few weeks, jot down things you can personally do to see the conflict in a more positive light.

Idea 2: Mine for conflict.

Writing prompt: Jot down a few ideas of areas where you might find some discrepancies between commitments and reality.

Idea 3: Acknowledge others who address conflict.

Writing prompt: Think of anyone who in the last two weeks has addressed conflict and who would be appropriate for you to acknowledge for their efforts. Write their names in the space provided with a brief description of the issues they addressed. Then go acknowledge them!

Idea 4: Understand that conflict requires tough decisions.

Writing prompt: Jot down one tough decision facing you in the upcoming weeks. List all the specifics and details of the situation.

Decision-Making Process Template

Reread your notes from the last prompt in the "Writing Prompts for Developing Your Conflict-Framing Skills" tool (page 127) about a difficult decision you'll need to make in the next few weeks. Now use the following template to assist you in thinking through the four steps of the decision-making process. Write your specific notes for each of the steps. Begin at the bottom of the pyramid, where you can jot down your notes on why the decision must be made. Then move up to the second level, where you jot down notes for the small-group meetings. Then move up to the third and fourth levels to plan for the clarification and final decision meeting.

Step 4: Share the final decision. Bring clarity and reasons for the decision in the best interests of your school.

_____

_____

_____

_____

_____

Step 3: Lead your clarifying session for the full staff. Determine when and where to have the full-staff meeting. Jot down all pertinent information from your small-group meetings.

_____

_____

_____

_____

_____

Step 2: Conduct small-group sessions to gain as much input as possible. Map out your specific plan for meeting with your staff.

_____

_____

_____

_____

_____

Step 1: Discuss why the decision has to be made. Write your *why* here.

_____

_____

_____

_____

_____

Two Steps to Identify Undiscussables

In the discussion about reframing your ideas of conflict in this chapter, I also cautioned against creating any undiscussables with your staff. These are items or topics your staff learn not to bring up to you because they upset you or you simply aren't willing to listen to alternative ways of doing things. Use the following activity to assist you in understanding if there are any undiscussables that you're not aware of in your leadership.

Step 1

Think back through your career, and write down any undiscussables that come to mind from department or grade-level chairs, administrators, or district office personnel you've worked with. List them here.

Step 2

Carefully select two staff members you could speak with about any possible undiscussables with your own leadership. Always use two people so the burden is not on a single person. Explain that you're trying to grow in your leadership and want to know if there are any topics or things that staff members feel they cannot discuss in your presence. Meet twice. In the first meeting, explain what you're asking them to do for you. Give them a week, and then schedule the second meeting for them to share. Nothing in writing is required. You simply want them to feel open to share things verbally. Thank them for their time and responses. It takes courage to share your administrator's undiscussables! When they leave, jot down the information they shared with you. Then, after careful consideration, bring up those actual topics in appropriate ways to show they're no longer undiscussable.

CHAPTER 8
Hold People Accountable

Accountability is tough. There seems to be a desperate need for leaders who are accountable for their own actions and commitments and who can hold others accountable for theirs. Finding such leaders is a fundamental challenge that many organizations face (Molinaro, 2018). Organizations must have leaders who demonstrate accountability because without it, the organization isn't going to move forward (Molinaro, 2018).

Accountability is a two-way street. You want to know that you can count on your staff to do what they're supposed to do. And just like you, your staff members want to know that they can count on you to do what you have committed to do. You begin this work of accountability by holding yourself accountable. Rather than blame, or rationalize, or make excuses when you make mistakes, own them. Acknowledge any pain your mistakes may have caused, and make amends. Make things right. It goes back to the first essential leadership skill of building relationships by being trustworthy and vulnerable. When you hold yourself accountable for your actions and commitments, you model those qualities and behaviors. You're trustworthy. You're vulnerable. You're also able to inspire and motivate others when you're holding yourself accountable. Only then are you ready to hold others accountable too.

In this chapter, we will discuss three things to consider in your leadership related to accountability: (1) securing commitment from your staff, (2) developing parallel accountability, and (3) recognizing both quantitative and qualitative measures of accountability. Try to strengthen your understanding of the great benefits of being a truly accountable leader who builds a culture of integrity. And at the same time, establish a respectful and enjoyable place to work. Be knowledgeable about your local district's terms of employment, resulting from the latest collective bargaining agreement. Use your human resources support network when needed, and get started by making an intentional choice to not avoid this essential skill.

In my work with principals, as we talk about holding their staff members accountable, I get the sense that many of them try to avoid it. There are two statements I hear quite often. Both are concerning. The first statement is usually something like, "I just don't have the time and energy to deal with that situation right now." And the second one goes something like, "That's just the way that teacher is. She's always been like that, and nothing I say is going to change her behavior. I'm not going to waste any of my valuable time on that."

[handwritten margin note: Read and study the union contract. Know it for yourself.]

My reply is usually, "You *must* find time." It's essential to deal with these unhealthy behaviors in your school because they're affecting your other staff and they're affecting the way your students are learning. Leaders must hold staff members accountable for these behaviors, actions like being late to school, not having required student data ready for the meeting, or always having something negative to say about parents. If a teacher has always been that way—not having her required student data ready for the meeting, for example—maybe no leader has ever had the courage to confront her to let her know how her behavior is affecting the team. This is where your courage comes in to make it clear that her behavior is not acceptable any longer under your leadership.

Whenever I hear principals say they just don't have the time to deal with actions like a teacher consistently speaking negatively about parents, I believe many of them just don't want to take the necessary and difficult steps to develop their skill of holding people accountable. Don't be one of those principals. Start to tackle this tough skill now. Actually, you've already begun by building relationships with your staff members and addressing conflict in healthy ways. Now you're in a much better position to hone this skill of holding people accountable. Again, I know accountability can be hard. It means understanding how to push staff members forward, while supporting them, without enabling them. To begin, remember that you can't hold staff members accountable unless you have clarified the work you're asking them to do and they have a clear understanding of what you expect of them. Once you have done that work, you can move on to commitment.

Secure Commitment From Your Staff

Clarifying the work is one of the essential leadership actions discussed in part 1 (page 9). Your staff members can't commit until you have clearly presented the work—and their specific role within that work—to them. That's why the principal playbook is such an essential tool. It helps you establish specific goals for your school and for individual staff members, making your expectations clear and specific. You make certain you have heard the staff members' voices, and you acknowledge their concerns. When you do this, they are much more willing to agree to the work that lies ahead. As you develop these goals, you validate and develop your people.

The time you take to hear teachers' thoughts and concerns is important for individual staff members and for your teams. In my early years of being a principal, I didn't fully understand that people can disagree with one another during the planning stages and discussions but then pull together even if the final decision is not the one for which they were hoping. They can be heard, they can disagree, and they can still commit and move forward. Without clarifying goals and commitment to those goals, it's almost impossible for you to hold people accountable. You can't hold teachers accountable for something they never understood they were expected to do. It's critical to clear up any confusion and ambiguity your staff members may have. Don't move forward to accountability without first taking action for clarifying the work.

On one occasion, I was working with a high school principal and a district literacy coach who were trying to embed guided groups to help their first-year students struggling to read at grade level. The principal chose a few English teachers and a special education teacher for this new initiative. Some were struggling to accept the responsibility of learning and implementing the new guided groups. These teachers needed training. It was clear that too many first-year students were not reading at grade level, but learning how to facilitate guided groups was really difficult work. Once the principal shared the reasoning, presented his data, and discussed expectations, all the teachers agreed to incorporate the new strategy. They would collect data and analyze student growth throughout the semester. I'll never forget what the principal did at the end of the meeting. He went around the room, saying this to each teacher, "I know it's going to be a lot of work. I will be here to give you the training and support you need. But do you commit to me and our students that you'll give it your best effort to incorporate these guided groups so our students will grow and advance in their literacy skills? Do you commit that we will not settle for this low standard any longer?"

It was amazing to watch for those few minutes. That meeting got really quiet once teachers realized what he was doing. He would look each teacher in the eye and ask the questions. After the teacher responded, he looked down at his paper and put a checkmark by that teacher's name. Then he raised his head and asked the next teacher. Each one of them committed. And all of them knew their principal was serious about the work ahead. They had committed to the training and the implementation plan. And they knew he would hold them accountable to their part in that commitment.

Let's look at one more example. When I served as middle school director, we had begun a mathematics initiative with a focus on helping students and teachers understand mathematics more conceptually. The state standards had changed and required much more conceptual teaching. Our district administrative team quickly realized we had another area where we needed a firm commitment from our teachers. In the particular mathematics framework we were using, there were five parts—(1) daily mathematics review, (2) conceptual teaching, (3) common formative assessments, (4) mathematical fact mastery, and (5) problem-solving posters—to be embedded in classrooms. As district leaders, we were providing professional development for administrators and teachers on each component in that mathematics framework. When it came to the professional development on the piece of problem-solving posters, we began to have an issue determining how often teachers needed to implement this strategy. With the problem-solving posters strategy, students used their previous learning to work through a complex mathematics problem. This strategy could take fifty minutes (an entire period), and sometimes, at least until we got the technique down, it could take some additional classroom time in the following class period too. Our district leadership asked teachers to use the problem-solving strategy every other Friday. This really upset some teachers. The new state standards were rigorous, and they felt like the strategy would simply take up too much of their instructional time. Some teachers didn't understand that the strategy itself involved essential time for instruction and error analysis. We had a decision to make. We had to decide how often we would require the problem-solving posters strategy. Once a quarter? Twice a quarter? Or four times a quarter as recommended?

After much discussion, we made the decision to try the strategy every other Friday. We asked each mathematics teacher to commit to that goal. Even though several of them were

Start with the why, then the how, followed by the what

hesitant and didn't think it would be an effective use of their time, each of them committed to the trial quarter. It was extremely important to them that we had consistent conversation and revisited the initiative at the end of the quarter, and we did. We learned that several teachers did not thoroughly understand the complexities of the problem-solving poster strategy. We learned that some of them needed more development in the mathematics concepts themselves, since we were trying to teach them conceptually, so we slowed down. Those teachers helped me understand that professional development was necessary before each problem-solving poster so that they felt competent and comfortable enough in their own skills.

At the end of the trial quarter, district leaders and the mathematics teachers decided to move forward with only two problem-solving posters each quarter. We debriefed after each one to see what went well and what didn't. By the next semester, several teachers who felt more comfortable with the strategy volunteered to do four per quarter even though it wasn't required. If people feel heard, if they know there is a plan when things don't go well, and if they trust in their leadership, people will commit—even to the difficult but necessary work.

Commitment is essential for accountability purposes. Before you ask people to commit to doing something (the what), you must be certain you have answered the question of why you're asking them to do it. It is critical to start with the *why* and move on then to the *how* and finally to the *what* (Sinek, 2009). Sinek's model of the Golden Circle (shown in figure 8.1) provides a visual representation of this concept. In this model, you begin in the inner ring with the why and work your way outward through the how and finally the what. Sometimes, leaders wonder why teachers don't get excited, jump right on board, and commit quickly with new initiatives. One explanation is that leaders do not begin with the why of the initiative or give that discussion enough time. They start right in with how they're going to do things and exactly what each staff member should be doing.

There will be times when you will struggle to gain your teachers' commitment on projects and initiatives unless you start with a strong why and give it the adequate time it needs for discussion and questions. I learned this the hard way.

The New Albany Floyd County district had begun a new literacy initiative of embedding guided groups for grades K–4 and had selected a specific framework for all elementary teachers to begin using in their instruction. Training and lots of professional

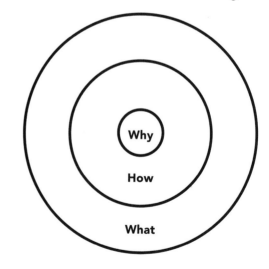

Source: *Adapted from Sinek, 2009.*

Figure 8.1: The Golden Circle.

development took place throughout the semester. The author of this particular program even came and provided personal consulting to the elementary teachers. Things seemed to be going well at the elementary level, and students who were still struggling to read at grade level received an additional guided group during intentional intervention time each day. They were making gains.

Then it was my turn, as director of the three large middle schools, to transition the initiative up through grades 5–8. I began attending the professional development sessions on the newly aligned literacy program, created a timeline for implementation, purchased all the resources teachers would need, and was even able to hire a literacy coach to assist the schools in implementation. I worked really hard. As a former secondary English teacher, I had no idea what to do when a student was unable to read at grade level. This work invigorated me to learn and grow in the specific techniques and strategies to help students read. I worked on every detail to have things ready for teachers. I wanted no questions to go unanswered as to the steps to begin, the materials to use, and how to set up the interventions for struggling students.

On the day of the training with the fifth- and sixth-grade ELA teachers, things seemed to go well. I explained that our goal was to align the school district with one literacy program for grades K–8 so students were using common language and strategies as they moved from one grade to the next, one school to another school, or one teacher to another teacher. The reading program was consistent. And when they struggled, teachers could work together to find solutions since they would all be using the same method. I explained that the district's elementary schools were already using this program. Then I presented the implementation timeline, gave out the resources, and discussed the upcoming training. The groups of thirty teachers were nice to me. They seemed a bit overwhelmed, and I worried that no one seemed as excited as I was, but I tried to push that concern out of my mind.

Then Doug called. Doug was a fifth-grade ELA teacher and served as the middle school representative and leader in our teachers association. Doug and I had a strong working relationship, spoke honestly with each other, and tried to solve issues together. But when I heard his voice, I knew he was concerned. He asked to stop by my office that afternoon. When he arrived, he said that the fifth- and sixth-grade teachers understood we needed to align the literacy program and that they felt good about the implementation plan. But he said that several teachers were confused and wondered why we were doing the guided groups program. I reiterated all my reasons from the morning meeting and reminded him that we needed to be able to monitor reading levels more accurately to have a smoother transition between grades. We wanted to make things less confusing for our students, who were currently getting different programs depending on which teachers they were assigned.

I've never forgotten Doug's response: "We understand why we need to align as a district, but we don't understand *why* this particular literacy program was chosen. You've hurt people's feelings. Some of them have been using other literacy frameworks for years and getting solid results. They don't know why the new one is going to be better than what they've been doing. Some of them feel like you don't think their work has been any good."

I sat back in my chair. He was right. I had worked so hard at explaining why we needed to align the program that I had never even thought about explaining why we needed *this* program. To be honest, I didn't know why this particular framework had been chosen.

I knew the elementary literacy coaches had done an extensive investigation to find the most beneficial program, so that program was what we'd use at the middle school level. But I had hurt teachers. And I felt awful. I thanked Doug for dropping by and sharing the concern. I apologized and said I'd get to work on getting the answer he needed.

A few days later, I was ready to give the reasoning behind the selection of that literacy framework and that specific method of doing guided groups. I left the district office to go visit each of the three middle schools and meet with the teachers again. Alongside their principal, I apologized for not having explained the why of the framework at the previous meeting. Some teachers didn't agree with the selected choice, but most all of them were willing to jump on board and get going after they had their questions answered. And I was able to talk with them on ways they could incorporate some of the strategies they were currently using into the new expectations. This process of sharing the why was challenging, but I was energized by the response from teachers once they felt heard and their questions were answered.

You must have the why, how, and what ready to go when asking staff members to engage in new work. It is critical to begin with the why. And I learned it's even more critical to make certain you're prepared to answer each and every *why* that your teachers and staff need in order to have the answers they deserve. If you expect people to commit, you must give them all the information and insight they need.

Once teachers have committed to the goals and initiatives, you must hold those teachers accountable to their commitments. You've set clear expectations. Now you follow up to make certain those expectations are met.

Develop Parallel Accountability

Many principals, because of their job title, think of accountability as an obligation only they have; they think they must hold themselves accountable, and everyone in their school too. But accountability doesn't need to solely lie with you, a single individual. Yes, you will hold yourself accountable. Yes, you will hold teachers accountable. But at the same time—running parallel to your efforts of accountability—teachers will hold each other accountable. Sometimes, these teachers work together in the same grade level or department, or on the same project or initiative. That's parallel accountability.

You work hard to help your teams grow and evolve, moving away from a top-down structure and into a horizontal structure where teams can become more accountable to one another. Your teams learn to not only collaborate and support each other but also hold each other accountable so they move forward into greater achievement. For example, when grade-level teams meet to discuss their data on the latest formative assessment and one teacher consistently comes unprepared with his students' data, the team members discuss the situation with that teacher. They hold him accountable for his responsibility to bring the data, just as each of them is doing. They know his behavior affects student learning and the work of their team. They are willing to hold each other accountable. There's no need to report this behavior to the principal unless it continues to occur after the team has spoken with him about the situation.

Prepare to answer each and every why

Parallel accountability is the goal. But that goal must start with you setting the example of holding people accountable. Because you've set clear goals and expectations and gained commitment, it becomes much easier to hold your staff members accountable for those goals. You spend the necessary time observing instruction, attending meetings, and reviewing data together to see if they are actually meeting the goals. You, as principal, are the key person to hold staff members accountable. Again, your goal is to demonstrate accountability so that teachers can grow and learn to hold each other accountable. Your goal is to develop strong grade-level and department teams so that they can work together and hold each other accountable to the work of your school.

But most often, teachers don't hold each other accountable because they don't see their principal holding teachers accountable. Teachers deserve to see their administrator as part of the process in establishing the curricular goals and expectations. Teachers deserve to have their principal aware of their commitment to those goals. And teachers deserve to see their principal holding each of them accountable to those commitments.

Teachers who *are* true to their commitment and follow through with the details of implementation can become disheartened when their principal doesn't do the same. When accountability is lacking, resentment builds because the principal is not holding everyone to the same level of performance. Mediocrity sets in because teachers realize it doesn't really matter if they do what's expected or not. It doesn't matter if they are true to their commitment or not. The responsibility of holding people accountable shouldn't entirely rest on you, as principal. But until you lead the way in holding others responsible for their goals and commitments, it's very unlikely that your staff will hold one another accountable. Teachers are watching you closely. They want and need to see you setting goals, confronting issues that arise, discussing difficult areas of implementation, and continuing to hold true to accountability. Simply put, if you're not holding teachers accountable, you're losing trust with some of your most valued teachers. If you continue to accept excuses, you'll continue to accept low standards. When you hold someone accountable, it means you care enough about that person and the school to not settle for mediocrity.

Parallel accountability begins with you. When you hold your staff accountable, they develop the skills to hold one another accountable too.

Recognize Both Quantitative and Qualitative Measures of Accountability

Something to keep in mind as you build your skill of holding people accountable is there are two measures of accountability: (1) quantitative and (2) qualitative. *Quantitative accountability* can be counted and measured using numbers. *Qualitative accountability* is descriptive and conceptual. Quantitative measures include things like teachers' common formative assessment data, grade distribution data, discipline referral data, completion of required curricular initiatives, professional development attendance, and so on. More curricular examples would include the number of times the teachers incorporated the problem-solving poster, or the guided groups, or other required items. Along with those actual numbers, you use student work examples and artifacts too.

Quantitative measures feel easier to use in assessing how teachers are doing with their instruction. For instance, if you've set an expectation for embedding the problem-solving poster strategy four times each quarter, then you can, through observations, make certain that teachers are doing so. You can also examine student work to see how students are performing. In your data meetings, you have plenty of information to use in measuring and holding teachers accountable.

For most principals, holding people accountable for qualitative measures is more difficult. Qualitative measures often involve actions of teachers and other staff members toward new projects; staff members' behavior in meetings; and staff members' communication with students, parents, team members, and other staff. These measures feel more subjective. They're messier. But holding staff accountable to qualitative measures can have a huge trickle-down effect for staff. Consider these two examples of qualitative accountability: (1) the teacher who's sarcastic and hurting team members with his words and (2) the team member who shares only negative comments in meetings and conversations with other teachers. When these behaviors are allowed to continue, the health of the school deteriorates. Addressing these issues is tough and uncomfortable. But when you realize that these actions are hurting staff members and causing negative emotions to spread throughout your school, you know it is wrong *not* to address the issues. It's easier to let them go, but that's detrimental to the health of your staff. Your school can't be truly healthy with those kinds of actions taking place. Addressing these behaviors through the real dialogue model (figure 6.1, page 110) can be invaluable. Continue to hone your skill of holding people accountable.

In my mind, the critical aspect of accountability is simple. Principals work so hard to create pacing guides, instructional goals, and expectations for learning. They put detailed plans into place, and then things seem to unravel and fall apart. Sometimes, they fall apart slowly, piece by piece. Sometimes, they fall apart almost immediately when people don't do what they commit to do. Principals must work just as hard at holding people accountable as they do in creating the expectations. Take an item from your systems list; let's use your teacher improvement plan as an example. If you, along with your team's input, take the necessary time to create a well-thought-out teacher improvement plan with clear goals, specific expectations, and a detailed timeline, you must follow through with holding the teachers accountable to the plan. Creating a plan for the teachers' improvement becomes meaningless if you don't follow up on each requirement of the plan. The work of building your systems does not create a healthy and structured learning environment if you're not disciplined enough to hold people accountable to the work of each system.

I had the opportunity to visit a school with a high percentage of student poverty that was attaining a high percentage of student achievement. I was eager to interview the teachers to see exactly how the school was reaching this incredible accomplishment. The teachers' comments were honest, open, and often included things about being held accountable. Comments from "Teacher A" offer an example:

> Our principal is very driven. He expects every student to grow and make learning gains each year. He really wants our school to be successful, and because he's so motivated, it motivates our staff, too. We work hard in the spring and some

during the summer so we're ready to go on day one. But we work as a team. Our principal knows exactly what our current student achievement scores are in our data rooms. He meets with us, is part of the conversation, and is not afraid to have the difficult conversations when needed. He will discuss where improvement is needed in certain areas, talk with specific teachers about an action plan, and then follow up with them in a few days. Yes, he sure does follow up. You can count on it. The issue will always be addressed. But he doesn't give us the answers for improvement. He'll give us the support we need, but he is clear that he expects us to be the professionals and figure it out. He believes we're the experts. So we'll go to other teachers in our department and look for strategies so that when he comes back, we have answers and things we're trying in our instruction. Because, like I said, you know he'll be back. He always follows up! It's common knowledge in our community. If you don't want to work hard on focused goals and grow together as a team, then this isn't the school for you. You can't hide here and do mediocre work. It's simply not allowed to happen. You'd need to go to some other school if you're not willing to work and grow. He has high expectations and he holds us accountable in every way.

Accountability is critical. When you hold your staff accountable for doing the clarified work, it multiplies trust among the individuals and teams in your school. Your staff can count on you; your staff can count on each other. Make certain you're honing your skill of accountability each day.

To reflect on holding people accountable and begin work on your next steps, see the reproducible tools on pages 140–142.

Writing Prompts for Developing Your Skill of Holding People Accountable

Review each of the three areas to consider when holding people accountable. Then in the space provided, write down a few sentences in response to each writing prompt.

Area 1: Secure commitment from your staff.

Writing prompt: Think of several situations in the next semester where you will need to make expectations clear and get commitment from your staff. Jot them down with any ideas you have.

Area 2: Develop parallel accountability.

Writing prompt: Think of situations where you have specifically held teachers accountable. Then think of any situations where teachers have held each other accountable. Write down why you think these teachers are able to hold each other accountable. Do they also hold their students accountable? How do they do that specifically? What are some ways you could help spread this parallel accountability throughout your school?

Area 3: Recognize both quantitative and qualitative measures of accountability.

Writing prompt: Describe two situations where you need to hold staff members accountable for quantitative measures. Then describe two situations where you need to hold staff members accountable for qualitative measures. Get specific about ways you will do this.

Source: Adapted from Sinek, S. (2009). Start with why: How great leaders inspire everyone to take action. *New York: Portfolio.*

Start With Why Template

As the leader of your school, you will have situations where you will need to share with your staff the reasons why you and they will be doing a certain initiative or project. Use the following template to sketch out your ideas and reasonings in the innermost circle. Then jot down the details of how and what. Share these initial thoughts with your leadership team to get feedback and strengthen each component.

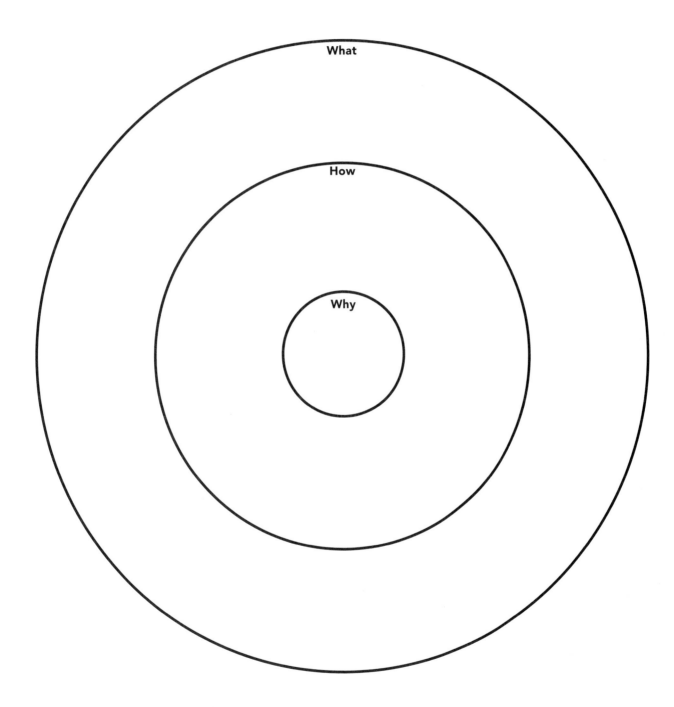

Source: Adapted from Sinek, S. (2009). Start with why: How great leaders inspire everyone to take action. *New York: Portfolio.*

Accountability Checklist and Reflection

Let's take a closer look at the quote from "Teacher A" from my research interviews, who describes her principal on page 138 at the close of chapter 8. Carefully, read each sentence based on that teacher's quote. Several of them deal with the principal's accountability skill. Take a few minutes to reflect on the sentence and consider if your staff could say the same thing about *your* leadership. If your answer is yes, then place a checkmark in the column labeled Yes, My Staff Would Say This Describes Me.

Accountability Reflection Statements	Yes, My Staff Would Say This Describes Me
Our principal is driven.	
Our principal expects every student to grow and make learning gains.	
Our principal really wants our school to be successful.	
Because our principal is motivated, our staff is motivated too.	
Our principal knows the current student achievement scores in our data rooms.	
Our principal meets with us (individually and as a team) and is part of conversations.	
Our principal is not afraid to have the difficult conversations when needed.	
Our principal discusses where improvement is needed in specific areas of our instruction.	
Our principal talks with teachers about an action plan where improvement is needed.	
Our principal follows up with teachers—always.	
Our principal always addresses issues.	
Our principal doesn't simply give us the answers to our improvement questions.	
Our principal gives us support but expects us to be the professionals and figure out a plan.	
Our principal believes we're the instructional experts.	
Our principal believes that if you don't want to work hard on focused goals and grow together as a team, then this isn't the school for you.	
Our principal doesn't allow us to do mediocre work.	
Our principal has high expectations and holds us accountable in every way.	

After completing the chart, see if there were any statements where you could not place a checkmark in the right column. Take a few minutes, reflect, and then write your thoughts on what actions you could take so that your staff *could* make those statements about you. Then add some of your own sentences that you would like your staff to say about your leadership accountability.

As you continue to hone these essential leadership skills—building relationships, reframing conflict, and holding people accountable—things can, at times, become really heavy. If you're anything like me, you're bound to have moments when you can't see the light at the end of the tunnel. There might even be times when you question your career path choice.

A principal can easily get caught up in negative parent phone calls, teacher issues, student discipline, and district office requests. More often than not, I think of myself as a really positive person, but I didn't always do a consistent job of handling the negative aspects of the work of being a principal. Sometimes, I allowed those negative aspects to be much higher on my priority list than they deserved to be. When someone was unhappy about something, I allowed that negativity to override the positive things going on in the school. Sometimes, I even began to allow myself to slip into thinking negatively or expecting the worst when I didn't have the actual facts of the situation. For example, when I was tired or frustrated and saw a group of teachers talking quietly together at the end of the hallway, I worried their conversation was about me. Maybe they were discussing something I was requiring them to do. I allowed those thoughts to enter my mind and worried about them when I had no idea if my thoughts were even accurate.

One other example of allowing myself to get caught up in the negative as a middle school principal would occur when receiving a call from the district office. When a message was left for me to return the call as soon as possible, I'd begin to panic just a bit. Sometimes, I would begin to prepare myself for the worst possible reasons for the call; things like being asked why teachers were making so many requests to transfer to other schools or being asked to explain why there were angry parents at the district office wanting to withdraw their students would pop into my head. Within a few short minutes, I'd come up with five or six horrible reasons the district office was calling.

During those days of allowing such negativity to overtake the positive, I even thought about going back into the classroom, where I knew I could be successful as a high school English teacher. But then something good would always happen at the school, and I'd be motivated once again to keep pushing ahead. The school and staff had exceptional things occurring. I couldn't allow one negative situation to hold me hostage from enjoying all

Just because you think do not make it true. your anxiet

those positives. For certain, I had to learn the skill of leaning into the positive and practice that skill on a consistent basis.

Leaders must lean into the positive aspects of the work. Psychology researcher Michelle Gielan (2015) suggests:

> Positivity is the world's most underutilized, natural occurring resource available to fuel success and forward progress. Too often our brains get caught up on all that is broken, forgetting about all that's working. . . . Leverage positivity and optimism to simultaneously activate the people around you and ignite positive change. (p. 27)

In this chapter, I will share and briefly introduce six tools to help you lean into the positive more consistently and not allow the negative to hold a dominant place in your leadership. Investigate and further study any tools that may resonate with you. You know to work hard on the right work. Now let's work just as hard at staying positive while doing that work. If you're going to create a positive environment in your school, you've got to maintain positive leadership within yourself. Being a healthy, strong, effective principal is never one single choice; it's a series of choices you make again and again. I hope using some of these tools will help you make those choices: (1) standing in the gap, (2) choosing a growth mindset, (3) holding the positive, (4) using the expectancy theory, (5) watching your emotions, and (6) priming your brain.

Tool 1: Standing in the Gap

I learned about this first tool, which is called *standing in the gap* (Hanig & Senge, 2015), at a conference session I attended. It looks something like figure 9.1.

Source: Adapted from Hanig & Senge, 2015.

Figure 9.1: Standing in the gap.

As a principal, you have so many things happening in your school throughout the day. When these situations occur, you have the choice to consider how you will think about each one. You can choose the negative route, moving to the left. Or you can choose the positive route, moving to the right. In that moment before you decide, you are standing in the gap; you have the opportunity to decide which way you'll allow your thinking to go. Using this model means you're doing the metacognitive work of thinking about your thinking. You're intentionally taking the time to notice your thoughts. If you recognize that you're thinking negatively for no real reason, you can choose to notice those negative thoughts, shift those thoughts to the positive side, and begin to handle the situation from a better vantage point. You're capable of rewiring your brain! It takes time, but with daily practice, it can be one of the most powerful tools you develop in your leadership.

My husband and I began using this tool together. We use it in our professional life and personal life as well. His feedback is invaluable to me. He says things like, "You're standing in the gap, but I think you're headed down the negative path." Most often, he's right. We spend time talking about what my triggering thoughts are in that particular situation and how I can notice those thoughts and stop them—actually stop them. I try to do the same for him. We have been working on this for a few years and have become so much better at noticing our negative thoughts and triggers and choosing the positive thinking instead.

We were traveling in Europe once and waiting to board a train. We both stopped and looked at each other when we heard the train officials yell out, "Mind the gap! Mind the gap!" These officials were referring to the gap between the platform and the moving trains. They were cautioning people to be careful, to pay attention, to be mindful of that gap so no harm came to anyone. Those same words are appropriate for you as you stand in the gap. Be mindful and pay close attention to your opportunity to get on the train moving in the right direction.

I'll never forget a consulting assignment where I worked with a middle school administrative team and discussed this tool. A few weeks after I introduced the tool, the principal interrupted a discussion the team and I were having about another topic to remind me of our work with this tool. He said, "Rhonda, you were standing in the gap and you went the wrong way!" We stopped what we were doing so he could share. The district's assistant superintendent had called the school that morning and asked for us to give her a call back that afternoon. She was new to the district, and the team's and my first session with her had been uncomfortable. I had quickly commented to the administrative team that I bet she was calling to say it would be my last day getting to coach and work with the team. She'd probably decided to go with another consultant. The principal looked straight at me and said, "I don't think so. Let's keep working, think about this positively, and then we'll handle what comes this afternoon when we return her call."

We did just that. We worked the rest of the day and accomplished several things. When we returned her call, she wanted us to know that she had heard some good results of our work together and wanted to join us at our next session. It was a little embarrassing for me. I had trained this principal to be aware of his thoughts and to choose the positive route. He had to remind me to practice what I was preaching. Train your brain. And don't think for a minute that your choices to move toward positivity do not impact your staff and your leadership.

Make a deliberate, intentional choice: when you're standing in the gap, move in the right direction. Lean into the positive.

Tool 2: Choosing a Growth Mindset

The second tool that can help you lean into the positive amid professional and personal circumstances is the work of committing to having a growth mindset. You will continually encounter roadblocks, disappointments, and situations that will frustrate you. The research of psychologist Carol Dweck (2017), known for her work on the mindset psychological trait, shows that "the view you adopt for yourself . . . can determine whether you become the person you want to be and whether you accomplish the things you value" (p. 6). A *mindset* includes the basic beliefs people have about their intelligence, talents, and personality. Working to build a consistent growth mindset should be the work of every principal.

Dweck (2017) continues by writing that mindset is not about picking up a few pointers here and there for your staff and students:

> It's knowing that every word and action sends a message . . . . It can be a fixed-mindset message that says: *You have permanent traits and I'm judging them.* Or it can be a growth-mindset message that says: *You are a developing person and I am committed to your development.* (p. 176)

With so much information readily available, many principals already have a solid knowledge base on the mindset research with a clear understanding of the fixed and growth mindsets. The Mindset Scholars Network, hosted at the Center for Advanced Study in the Behavioral Sciences at Stanford University, is a group of leading social scientists dedicated to improving student outcomes and expanding educational opportunity by advancing the scientific understanding of students' mindset about learning and school. One of its research briefs shares the importance of exposing students to the neuroscience evidence on the malleability of the brain so that students clearly understand intelligence is something each of them can develop and grow (Romero, 2015). Exposure to the neuroscience isn't just for students. All members of the school community—students, teachers, and educational leaders—can benefit greatly from understanding that effort is good and building resilience is a vital skill in life. As leaders, we all want our schools to be a warm, challenging, and engaging place for everyone to stretch and grow.

Generally speaking, people with fixed mindsets spend time documenting their intelligence and talents. They worry about their qualities and try to prove themselves to others. They believe they have fixed abilities and talents and need to work with those as best they can. On the other hand, people with growth mindsets spend time developing their intelligence and talents. They focus on making efforts to get even better; they know it takes time and hard work, and they persevere through setbacks. They believe their intelligence and talents are just the starting point. They welcome challenges and opportunities to improve. People with growth mindsets are resilient, flexible, open to learning new things, confident, optimistic, and ready for the long haul of work ahead.

My own experience has taught me that this commitment to having a growth mindset takes a lot of intentional effort and a lot of inward reflection, just as standing in the gap does. It goes hand in hand with the standing in the gap tool and also takes determined, daily choices to look for opportunities to tackle difficult things and grow. If the view you adopt about yourself profoundly affects the way you live your life, then this view most obviously affects the way you lead your school. Depending on the particular situation, I find myself flowing back and forth between growth and fixed mindsets. I've learned that some circumstances, and even certain people, can trigger me toward a fixed mindset. Again, just as with the standing in the gap tool, I'm continually working on my inner thinking to intentionally cultivate a more consistent growth mindset.

Leaning into the positive with a growth mindset means paying attention to learning new things and growing into a better leader. It's about strengthening your resilience when you mess up. It's about being willing to struggle to lead difficult work. It means you're willing to put in your own hard work, time, and effort to grow. And when something doesn't go exactly right, you try to accept the situation and begin looking for ways to learn from it and make the situation better. Growth mindset leaders don't allow their failures to define them or diminish them. Instead, they learn to dig deep and find strength when things are difficult. Maintaining a growth mindset is the ultimate decision of using your mistakes or failures to expand yourself into becoming a better leader and a better human being.

After exploring fixed and growth mindsets, you'll probably find yourself questioning your negative thoughts: "Why am I thinking this way? Why don't I stop these thoughts and look at other, more positive ways of seeing things?" Those questions are great indicators that you're thinking about your thinking! You'll also find yourself thinking about other people's thinking.

Once I learned about fixed and growth mindsets, I began listening in a new way to teachers' and other principals' comments about work they were doing in their schools. Without meaning to, my mind was categorizing their comments into fixed and growth mindsets. My thoughts would include things like, "Oh, he's got such a fixed mindset. He won't consider any other way of doing things except his own. He sure thinks he knows it all," or "She's got to understand that things aren't going to be perfect all the time and it's OK when she messes up." Dweck (2017) writes that sociologist Benjamin Barber must have felt similarly when he said, "I don't divide the world into the weak and the strong, or the successes and the failures . . . . I divide the world into the learners and nonlearners" (p. 16).

The same categorizing happens when I listen to comments that teachers make as they begin new initiatives. An example that comes to mind is when I was serving as our district's middle school director and we began a curricular project of writing rigorous curriculum design units in the middle school social studies and science departments. The why of the initiative was to align curriculum across all three middle schools with highly engaging and thought-provoking units for each grade level. Teachers would determine the essential standards, develop an engaging scenario, select the best and most rigorous activities, and create an authentic and demanding writing piece within each unit. The teachers were attempting to examine their instruction and determine the best of their best curricular strategies and lessons. Between the finalized, selected unit pieces, we provided time for teachers to incorporate some of their own lessons that were not selected for the district units.

It didn't take long in this process for the comments, and my mindset categorizing, to begin. First, some actual fixed-mindset comments: "I don't know why we can't just keep teaching what we've always used. If I wanted to use new ideas, I'd do that when I wanted." Mentally, I was making the checkmark beside the person's name. *Fixed.* "What's the quickest and easiest way to get this unit work finished?" *Fixed.* "My teaching stuff has worked for me all these years. I don't understand why I might want to use other teachers' ideas." *Fixed.* "Just tell us what you want, Rhonda. We don't need to get trained or go through a big professional development process together. Just divide the work up, and we'll figure it out and do our own part. That'll be quicker." *Fixed.* "I'm not clear on why we're required to have a writing component. That's what the English teachers do." *Fixed.* I could add several more here, but you get the gist.

And thankfully, there were the growth-mindset comments shining brightly among the fixed. "This work of unit development will help. I was needing some better ideas on a particular section of the Africa unit. I can't keep doing the same things. They haven't been working." *Growth.* "This is going to be a lot of change for me, but my teaching will be better in the end." *Growth.* "It's not ethical or fair to our students not to include the whole story, the truth of America's history." *Growth.* "Students will love these units! They'll be getting the best lessons from all of us. I should've been incorporating these years ago." *Growth.* "I had no idea other teachers were requiring so much from their students. I've got to step it up." *Growth.* "We're a team in this district now. Seven social studies teachers working together can write better lessons and incorporate better, more well-rounded resources than I can on my own." *Growth.*

It really surprised me to hear the fixed-mindset comments, but the growth-mindset comments were alive and well, and those were what I needed to encourage and strengthen. I needed to acknowledge the growth-mindset comments and build on each of them. I needed to assist some teachers in shifting over to a growth mindset and maintaining it as much as possible. Students' learning depended on it.

One caution that Dweck talks about is to be careful in saying you have a growth mindset. In other words, she suggests that you don't need to declare it if you don't have it (as cited in Talks at Google, 2015). Sometimes, your insights about your own mindset may not be accurate. People are quick to claim good things for themselves, like having a growth mindset, without doing the work or taking the journey that leads to having this mindset. A system that seems to provide an accurate read on leaders' and others' mindsets is the system of observation and evaluation. Think about how you and your staff react when receiving evaluative feedback. People with a growth mindset are open to accurate information about themselves. If they don't receive the feedback they were hoping for, they are able to accept that feedback and have the confidence in their ability to grow in any area needed. On the other hand, people with a fixed mindset often think highly of themselves and begin to believe they have a growth mindset even when it's not true. They struggle with any feedback not being at the highest ranking possible and consider any failure a major setback. They believe effort is a bad thing. They want to be the best immediately, without having to work. They waste time on making sure everyone knows how competent they are instead of actually getting better. They spend time and effort hiding their deficiencies instead of working on them. They want to be near people who console them instead of those who challenge them. These people can be seemingly positive people at times, until it comes to areas of improvement. They believe they have a growth mindset. They tell themselves and others as much. But they are mistaken and have much shifting to do.

As a principal, you can see these mindsets shine brightly as you lead your own curricular change, facilitate difficult and meaningful evaluation conversations, and receive your own evaluation recommendations from your supervisor. These are all opportunities for you to demonstrate and grow your positive mindset. They're chances for you to demonstrate as a leader that believing in your ability to grow and change is more important than believing in your own intelligence and capabilities.

A growth mindset is worth the work! I have found that in every aspect of life—my work as a principal, as a consultant, as a wife, as a mom, as a sister, and as a friend—a growth mindset has led to a much more enriched and rewarding existence. One of my sisters and I were shopping together one day and she pointed out a small wooden wall hanging with these words, "What you find in your mind is what you put there. Put good things there." That pretty much sums up this tool of choosing your mindset.

Make a deliberate, intentional choice: do the work of strengthening your growth mindset every day. Lean into the positive.

Tool 3: Holding the Positive

This next tool may surprise you a bit. It's about holding on to your positive thoughts. You might be asking yourself, "Why would I have to *try* to hang on to positive thoughts? It just makes sense to do that!" But that's not what our human brains are wired to do. Our brains have a negativity bias that causes us to hold on to negative experiences and quickly forget positive ones. Millennia ago, these hardwired brains of ours were critical to our survival as a species, but now they seem to be a source of anxiety and sadness (Hanson, 2013). Understanding why our brains lean toward the negative can help you look at your challenges and tough times with a new perspective. Rick Hanson (2014), founder of the Wellspring Institute for Neuroscience and Contemplative Wisdom, writes:

> [As] we evolved over millions of years dodging sticks (threats) and chasing carrots (food), it was a lot more important to notice, react to, and remember sticks than it was for carrots. That's because—in the tough environments in which our ancestors lived—if they missed out on a carrot, they usually had a shot at another one later on. But if they failed to avoid a stick—a predator, a natural hazard, or aggression from others of their species—WHAM, no more chances to pass on their genes.

It seems that this need for survival has caused us to hang on to negative thoughts and experiences much more than our positive ones.

An analogy I heard in discussing this idea of holding on to negative thoughts versus holding on to positive ones has stayed with me: the analogy of Velcro versus Teflon. Richard Rohr (2017), author and founder of the Center for Action and Contemplation, points out:

> Your mind wraps around the negative and holds on, like Velcro . . . the human mind is attracted to the negative. We have to choose the positive. Because when we have a positive thought . . . if you don't consciously hold on to that thought for a minimum of fifteen seconds, it does not imprint on the brain. It slides off like Teflon.

This Velcro and Teflon theory caused me to stop and take a serious look at my thoughts and what I actually hold on to myself. I've found that it is indeed easier to grab hold of negative thoughts and ideas. In fact, I've found that I am drawn to holding on to the negative thoughts, derogatory comments, and past circumstances. If I'm not conscious in my thinking, I can even help them grow and expand into even bigger and more powerful negative conversations inside my head. I've discussed this with other people, and it seems many of us enjoy hanging on to thoughts of being the victim of situations in our lives; we enjoy talking about how tough things are at work; we enjoy talking about the flaws of people we don't like; we enjoy making comparisons to other people. We could go on and on with our negative chatter. Sometimes, the chatter stays inside our minds, and sometimes, we speak it out loud. And when others join in the negative thoughts, things really get going, and we soak up all the negativity. Our negative thoughts cling to our brains, without any work on our part, like soft things cling to Velcro.

Yet when it comes to our positive thoughts, these seem to slide out of our minds as if our brains were coated with Teflon. Try intentionally holding on to a positive thought for approximately fifteen seconds in order for it to stay in your mind. Your positive thoughts need time to travel from your short-term memory to your long-term storage. When negative thoughts or negative conversations arise throughout the day, practice letting them pass by and move on through your brain. Practice not grabbing your negative thought and perseverating on it. Practice not joining in the conversations about how bad things are or any negative talk about other people. Practice holding on to a positive thought, thinking about it a few seconds longer, giving value to the thought, writing it down, and maybe sharing it with someone else. Practice rewiring your thinking. Practice until the positive thoughts stick like Velcro and negative ones slide right off.

I've seen so many principals consistently show appreciation to their staff members through positive, kind gestures. These principals keep a box of thank-you notes in their desk to leave handwritten notes, some of which may hang on display by teachers' desks for years. They keep chocolate, candy, and flavored waters in stock to share with staff. They use these strategies to maintain a positive environment. Now, along with these positive acts of kindness, let's all start to hold on to our positive thoughts too.

Make a deliberate, intentional choice: hold on to your good, positive thoughts, and make them stick. Lean into the positive.

Tool 4: Using the Expectancy Theory

As I begin to discuss the fourth tool that could assist you in your work of intentionally leaning into the positive, I want to quickly define the expectancy theory. This theory, first proposed in 1964 by business professor and organizational behavior expert Victor H. Vroom, is based on factual evidence that the brain is organized to act on what it predicts will happen next. Achor (2011), in writing about the theory, suggests:

> What this means in the workplace is that beliefs can actually change the concrete results of our effort and our work . . . The expectation of an event causes the same complex set of neurons to fire as though the event were actually taking place. (p. 70)

What you believe will happen can actually change the results you get.

Achor (2011) cites a study in which Harvard researchers Alia J. Crum and Ellen J. Langer (2007) told half the workers at seven hotels how their daily work was creating an abundance of exercise for them. They shared how many calories the daily activity was burning and how vacuuming is similar to cardio workouts. The researchers made certain to well inform these workers of the impact their work was having on their bodies. They prepared this half of the workers for the research study by having them think about these benefits before their work began for the upcoming week. The researchers held no such conversation with the other half of the workers; their work went on as usual. The study found that the workers who had awareness of the benefits and knowledge of the possible impact of their work actually lost weight and lowered their cholesterol levels. The workers who did not hear about all the positive benefits of their work had no change in health results. The only difference between the two groups' working conditions was how their brains were thinking about their work. The researchers' fundamental conclusion was that the mental construction of your daily activities, more than the activities themselves, defines your reality (Achor, 2011; Crum & Langer, 2007). Wow! Think about the specific implications this could have for you as you lead your school.

First, you must begin to think of your own work in the most positive light and acknowledge the difference your work is making. And second, you must help develop mental constructs around the work your teachers are doing in their classrooms each day. It's your responsibility to verbalize your appreciation for their hard work, especially in difficult instructional changes, and your belief that it will make a difference in students' learning. When using this expectancy theory, you can begin doing the intentional work of making certain that teachers know how much their daily work impacts the school and students. You make certain that teachers know you're well aware diagnosing each student's particular learning needs is extremely difficult work. You show more appreciation for those teachers doing that intensive work. You make it a priority to expect the best from teachers and to help them expect the best too. You are building and solidifying strong mental constructs for your own daily work and your teachers' work.

When I was principal at Scribner Middle School, a teacher wrote me a note but decided not to give it to me as she had planned. I'm glad she didn't. Here's why.

It was a Monday afternoon after a hectic morning at school. I stopped by this teacher's classroom and had an honest one-on-one conversation with her about her literacy training with other teachers and all her hard work. I had designed her schedule so that she worked with small groups of students throughout the day, trying to improve their deficient areas and assist them in reading at higher levels. I knew I was asking a lot of her to diagnose students' individual needs, collaborate with other secondary teachers, and assist the teachers in gaining ground with their own literacy abilities. It would have been much easier for her to have a schedule of six periods of regular English. It would have been much easier to just think, "If students can't read, tough luck."

I stopped by her classroom that afternoon to let her know how much I appreciated her professionalism in the literacy development, her attempts at facilitating the small groups, and her perseverance through this challenging work. I told her I couldn't wait to see her students' results in three more weeks on the next official assessment and data review date. She was facing big challenges, and I wanted to make certain she knew how much her work mattered. She was rising to the challenge. She listened to my words, stood there for a moment without saying a word, and then thanked me for stopping by.

Three weeks later, in that next assessment and data review meeting, her results were higher than any of the other teachers'. All but one of her students had made gains. And here's the point of the story: After that meeting, she stopped by my office to let me know just how much my words of encouragement and belief in her work had meant to her. Then she handed me the note she had written before my initial meeting with her. It was a note telling me of her plan to resign her position at the end of the semester and return to a position at an elementary building. She shared that she had come to a place where she didn't believe in herself or her teaching abilities. She knew our school had to do something to help the students read. She knew I had high expectations of her. But she didn't believe in herself to meet those expectations. She simply didn't believe her instruction was making a difference. However, she didn't give me the note that day I stopped by—she kept it in her drawer—because my words to her began to change her way of thinking. She began to believe in her intentional and focused work and began to think she might get better results than she thought. She began to believe in herself too. Because I expected her to do well, she worked even harder and expected to do well herself. Her daily instructional strategies didn't change. But the mental constructs of believing in herself and her hard work did. And the results came.

I'm so glad she shared that note with me. The experience led me to begin making a concerted effort at giving focused feedback to teachers while sharing my belief in their abilities. When people know what you expect, know you believe in their abilities, and know results should come, they can begin to believe in their own abilities and expect the same results. You believe they can get results. Each of them must believe in their abilities to get results too.

Make a deliberate, intentional choice: expect good results from yourself and your staff. Build solid mental constructs. Lean into the positive.

Tool 5: Watching Your Emotions

Watching your emotions. Those are three powerful words. People need to know that you, as a leader, are in control of your emotions so they can continue to build trust and confidence in you and your leadership. This fifth tool can help you, as a principal, see the importance of watching your emotions in two ways: (1) watching your emotions so that you don't get hijacked by them and emotionally shut down and (2) watching your emotions so that you mirror positivity. I read a sentence once that I've never forgotten: "Your energy introduces you before you even speak" (Wright, 2018). Your energy, the emotions you carry with you, is dynamic and people can sense your energy when you step into a room. When leaders' energy is negative, staff feels it. When their energy is positive, staff senses that too.

Jill Bolte Taylor, author and Harvard professor, suffered a brain hemorrhage in the left hemisphere of her brain while getting ready for work one day. While in the hospital after the hemorrhage, she noticed there were two kinds of people coming in and out of her hospital room: (1) people who brought her energy and (2) people who took her energy away. She desperately needed people who could bring hope and energy to her. She needed people to take responsibility for the kind of energy they brought into her recovery room. She needed people to consciously walk into her room, to show up for her, and to not bring any bad energy. She was keenly aware of who was there to help her and who was there to simply go through the motions of their work (as cited in Super Soul Sunday, 2011).

Clearly, as leaders we need to take responsibility for the emotional energy we bring to our schools. Let's look at emotional hijacking and mirroring. Emotional hijacking can occur when people become so caught up in the emotion of the situation that they simply react without thinking about their reaction. Think about situations in your school where staff members, parents, and even you reacted in a negative way. Maybe you got caught up in the moment or were tired and frustrated. It's critical to remember that, as Goleman (2019) suggests, a leader's emotional self-regulation really matters. And why does it matter so much? According to Goleman (2019):

> First of all, people who are in control of their feelings and impulses . . . are able to create an environment of trust and fairness. In such an environment, politics and infighting are sharply reduced and productivity is high. Talented people flock to the organization and aren't tempted to leave. And self-regulation has a trickle-down effect. No one wants to be known as a hothead when the boss is known for her calm approach. Fewer bad moods at the top mean fewer throughout the organization. (pp. 28–29)

The ability to self-regulate your emotions, avoiding an emotional hijacking, is a critical skill. Allowing your emotions to rule can take a toll on you as a leader. When small stresses pile up and you have entirely too much on your plate, it's very easy to lose control. You may begin speaking with your feelings and emotions, and your colleagues clearly see it. You may lash out at other people, you may withdraw into yourself and not communicate, or you may do both. But one thing is certain: it's not healthy for your school. Motivation and productivity can be lost. Clear decisions can be difficult to make. And relationships can deteriorate. You must be aware if you become hijacked by your emotions so you can let people know. It's OK to say, "I'm getting emotionally tired. Let's take a break."

This emotional hijacking topic came up in a feedback session of mine. I had asked two well-respected staff members to consider any blind spots in my leadership. This exercise is my adaptation of the work and concepts in the Johari Window, developed by Joseph Luft and Harrington Ingram. The Johari Window invites you to reflect about yourself and invite feedback from others. This feedback allows you to discover strengths, weaknesses, and blind spots, which are behaviors and actions you may not be aware of (Explorance, 2020). I didn't want them to speak with other staff about this. I just wanted the two of them to meet and think of one or two unproductive things I was doing in my leadership that I was probably not aware of—my blind spots. I knew I was asking a lot of them. Who wants to tell their leader, the person who writes their evaluations, where she could get better? But I had a deep level of trust in these two staff members, and they knew I was trying to grow as a leader.

Here's one of their conclusions: I sometimes became emotionally hijacked. They shared that when I got tired or frustrated in meetings, I would push my chair back from the table, get quiet, and look down. They said they, and several other staff members, were aware of my reaction and knew to back off a topic and let things settle when I reacted that way. Or sometimes, they just agreed to do whatever I was requesting.

What feedback! I had no idea I was doing this. Apparently, I wasn't saying much, but my body language and emotions were speaking volumes. The two staff members said it would be helpful if I would just express my frustration in meetings and tell them to move ahead with the conversation while I took a mental rest for a bit. They were capable of facilitating the conversation until I was ready to join back in. I've never forgotten that feedback, delivered to me in a kind and honest way. And I'm a better leader because of it. The three of us never spoke of it again. They both knew I took their words to heart because they saw my actions change.

Being aware of your emotions must be a priority because it affects your interactions with your staff. Achor (2011) explains that the relationship between you and the people who work with you is:

> the single most important social bond you can cultivate at work. Studies have found that the strength of the bond between manager and employee is the prime predictor of both daily productivity and the length of time people stay at their jobs . . . When this relationship is strong, companies reap the rewards. (p. 189)

Not only do you want to be able to self-regulate your emotions so you don't become emotionally hijacked, but you also want to have awareness of the emotions you exude and the effect they have on the people around you. The brain has mirror neurons that are "specialized brain cells that can actually sense and mimic the feelings, actions, and physical sensations of another person" (Achor, 2011, pp. 203–204). Stop and think about the incredible opportunities and responsibility of recognizing this phenomenon as a principal. The emotions that you bring and share within your school environment can—and will—be mirrored back to you in the same feelings, actions, and sensations.

Emotions are contagious, and every interaction you have with others has an emotional aspect to it. The contagion is subtle and almost imperceptible, but be assured that, as Goleman (2006a) writes, people "catch feelings from one another as though they were some kind of social virus" (p. 115). Whatever the communication between people, these exchanges can make individuals feel better, somewhat better, a little worse, or just awful. From each encounter, people can take that emotional mood and retain it for hours after the actual event. Conversations and encounters are like an emotional economy where you exchange good and bad like gains and losses (Goleman, 2006b). At the end of the day, you want your leadership to be part of facilitating more good exchanges, or gains, in your communication.

As the leader of your school, you want to exhibit good, positive emotions so your staff mirror good, positive emotions back to you. Another way to visualize your part in this, other than as a mirror, is to consider yourself as a television broadcaster. For two years, my undergraduate major was in journalism and broadcasting. Back then, I couldn't wait to become a news anchor, so that might be why this analogy, which Michelle Gielan (2015) presents in her book *Broadcasting Happiness: The Science of Igniting and Sustaining Positive Change*, resonates so much with me. Gielan (2015), who founded the Institute for Applied

Positive Research and is herself a former television news anchor, writes that leaders are all broadcasters, and they need to be positive broadcasters who deliver their messages with optimism. She writes that leaders must understand that what they broadcast predicts success. Leaders' words affect people. The messages they send can either lead their staff to see obstacles as unsurmountable or encourage them to see the challenges with possibilities and success (Gielen, 2016) Negative broadcasting, including gossip, negative frustrations, and finger pointing, can hurt schools. We need to broadcast positive messages so staff members can mirror them back to us and others.

Tom Hierck, educator and author on creating positive learning environments, sums it up well when he writes, "Whether you create it or you condone it, you own it" (Williams & Hierck, 2015, p. 93). The principal sets the tone for the building.

Make a deliberate, intentional choice: don't get hijacked by your negative emotions. Instead, mirror positive ones. Lean into the positive.

Tool 6: Priming Your Brain

This sixth and final tool is my favorite. It involves the idea of priming your brain with positive thoughts *before* performing a difficult task.

Several research experiments have been done with children and adults around this idea. Achor (2011) cites one experiment (Master, Barden, & Ford, 1979) that involved asking four-year-old children to put blocks together. Children in one group were asked to think about something happy before they began. That group of children significantly outperformed the other group, whose members were not asked to think about anything specifically (Achor, 2011). Another research experiment (Schmitz, De Rosa, & Anderson, 2009) involved showing adults a series of pictures and asking them to remember as much about the pictures as they could. Before seeing the pictures, some of the adults were asked to each think about one positive thought or circumstance for a few minutes. The other adults were asked to each think about a negative thought or situation for several minutes. Both groups were then shown the pictures. The group primed with negative thoughts couldn't recall substantial parts of the pictures' backgrounds. But the group primed with positive thoughts before viewing the pictures was able to visualize and recall much more (Achor, 2011).

These research experiments provide evidence that happy thoughts actually give your brain a chemical edge because these positive thoughts flood your brain with dopamine and serotonin (Achor, 2011). They make you feel good and enable your brain to think at higher levels. These chemicals also help you organize new information, retain it, and retrieve it more quickly when needed. You are able to be more creative, more innovative, more solutions focused, and more results driven.

This tool of priming your brain is one I put into practice as quickly as I could after reading and reflecting about it. I began pausing and taking a few moments to think of positive outcomes before difficult meetings. As a middle school director, I would shut my door for three to four minutes before tense central district committee discussion meetings. These were often difficult sessions where teacher representatives from each school came to discuss and address any concerns in their building or at their particular level: elementary, middle, or high school. I would intentionally take those few minutes to think about a couple of good things that our district was accomplishing. Or I would concentrate on one key factor that I knew would be a positive component for most everyone in the meeting. I would think of positive ways the meeting could flow. Before school board meetings, I began to sit in my car for a few moments and concentrate on good things happening in the middle schools.

Before speaking in front of groups in my consulting, I often find a quiet spot where I can stand for a moment by myself to breathe and get a few good thoughts in my mind. It helps. It really helps me prepare myself, think more clearly, and stay in a better frame of mind. I don't seem to get as frustrated or take things as personally when difficult topics arise. Prime yourself to allow positive thoughts to influence your behavior. Prime your brain to strengthen your leadership.

Make a deliberate, intentional choice: prime your brain with positive thoughts and images before a difficult situation. Lean into the positive.

Stay Positive

I don't know about you, but I certainly struggle at times to maintain a positive outlook on work and all the complex challenges it holds. These six tools are strategies I learned over the years and began embedding into my leadership. I hope one or two of them will resonate with you and enhance your ability to lean into the positive.

It's easy to narrow one's thinking by focusing on the problems and issues that leaders face. This focus on the difficulties and obstacles can lead to a negative, unproductive work environment. But when we broaden our thinking and intentionally look for the opportunities that lie within the challenges, we as leaders can create a much more positive and energizing spirit in our schools—for our students, our staff, and ourselves.

To reflect on leaning into the positive and begin work on your next steps, see the reproducible tools on pages 157–160.

Six Tools to Lean Into the Positive

Take some time to consider each of the tools from this chapter. Using the following template, record your answers to the questions on the left side, and then complete the right side by filling in ideas for ways you can use the tools.

Tool 1: Standing in the Gap	
Think about a specific time where you were standing in the gap. What did you do? Do you more often move in the positive or the negative direction?	Future possibilities for using this tool:

Tool 2: Choosing a Growth Mindset	
Reflect on your own mindset. Currently, which is your predominant mindset—growth or fixed? And what are some recent situations where you heard the mindsets of your teachers and staff members?	Future possibilities for using this tool:

Tool 3: Holding the Positive	
Jot down two good things that happened this week in your school. Stop. Sit in the silence for a few minutes, and reflect on those positive things. Hold on to those thoughts for several minutes. Allow them to attach onto your brain like Velcro.	Future possibilities for using this tool:

Tool 4: Using the Expectancy Theory

Think of one specific staff member who is doing rigorous work and who you want to make aware of the impact of that work. Remind yourself that the mental constructs teachers have about their work are powerful pieces of how students learn in their classrooms. How will you assist this teacher in knowing and expecting the best from his or her work?	Future possibilities for using this tool:

Tool 5: Watching Your Emotions

Take a few minutes to think of your emotions the last few days. Were there any instances of hijacking where you felt you didn't handle things in the best way? Jot them down. Can you think of instances where you intentionally mirrored positive emotions? Jot them down.	Future possibilities for using this tool:

Tool 6: Priming Your Brain

Choose one upcoming situation that will most likely involve some difficult or negative details. This could be a difficult staff meeting, an IEP conference, a parent meeting, a data discussion meeting with a department, or a district meeting or conversation. Begin to prime your brain. Think of everything you can do to prepare for the situation. Begin to envision the positive results and outcomes that could potentially occur.	Future possibilities for using this tool:

Leading With Positive Tools Rating Chart

As you begin to embed the tools from this chapter into your daily practice, use the following template to assess your current ability to use each tool. In the second column, rate your current ability to use the tool with an E for emerging (I'm working on this tool); a C for competent (I feel adequate in using this tool, but could get better); or a P for proficient (I feel competent with this tool and use it regularly). In the third column, provide a couple of reasons for that rating, and in the fourth column, record your next steps for gaining more confidence in using the tool. Of course, there's no need to complete the fourth column if you rated yourself proficient with a tool.

Tool	Rating of Your Current Ability: E = Emerging C = Competent P = Proficient	Reasons for Your Current Rating	Next Steps for Increasing Your Confidence in Using This Tool
Ability to move in the positive direction when standing in the gap			
Ability to consistently sustain a growth mindset and help your staff grow in their mindsets			
Ability to consistently hold on to positive thoughts and release negative ones			
Ability to expect the best and build the mental constructs for your staff			
Ability to mirror strong positive emotions instead of becoming hijacked by negative ones			
Ability to stop and prime your brain before difficult meetings, conversations, and situations			

Holding the Good Stuff: Two Simple Steps

If you'd like to do some additional work on holding the positive (a tool to help with decreasing the brain's negativity bias), take some time to focus on the positive things in your life. Each time you do this—reflect on positive experiences—you make a difference in your thinking, and those differences add up to the reshaping of your brain.

Step 1: Take opportunities throughout the day to stop and notice small, positive things around you.

Notice things like the taste of good coffee, the breeze in the air, the sun shining brightly, your favorite song playing, a smile from a stranger, and so on. When you notice something positive, allow yourself to feel good about it. Keep opening up to these thoughts. Stop and take notice of these positive things throughout the day. In the space provided, write down a few positive things from your day.

Step 2: Stop and actually savor a positive experience from your day.

When you have a good experience during your day, try to sustain or stay with that experience for twenty to thirty seconds. Many times people get distracted by something else. Try to stop and actually feel the positive experience in your body and through your emotions. Then at the close of each day, intentionally reflect on one positive experience from your day. The experience could be something like someone giving you a compliment, an achievement of a staff member, taking a walk outside after work, your own child doing something to make you smile, and so on. Think about this positive experience again for twenty to thirty seconds. The longer that you hold something in your awareness, the more neurons that fire and wire together to create a stronger network in your memory. Take a few minutes and write down a few sentences about your one positive experience from the last twenty-four hours.

Source: Adapted from Hanson, R. (2014) Taking in the good vs. the negativity bias. *Accessed at www.sfsu.edu/~holistic /documents/Spring_2014/GoodvsNeg_Bias.pdf on June 19, 2021.*

CHAPTER 10

Turn Inward

All chapters in this book have focused on essential actions or skills needed to be an effective principal. This final chapter on turning inward may be the most important. This skill is what makes all the other skills and actions possible. It's about looking at your leadership, reflecting on it, and finding ways to make it even better.

This final chapter is a short one. Hopefully, its brevity will allow you to take a step back, slow down your breathing, and think about the importance of your work. The role of being a principal is overwhelming. The work is never done. Some principals never stop or slow down enough to take an inward look. Many principals are overscheduled, tired, and feeling guilty for what they *aren't* doing at school and at home. Too often, amid this heavy workload, I hear principals say, "I've got this. I can do it." They're stuffing down emotions, building pressure within, and ultimately struggling to hold everything together. They and you must look inward and care for yourselves. It's impossible to pour from an empty glass. You must find specific ways to model self-care and take the necessary time to release the pressure and fill your cup so you can lead well.

In this chapter, we'll look at three strategies, with the research to back them, that may help with your self-care. They've certainly helped me. These are not the physical workouts that many of us use and benefit from, like lifting weights, doing yoga, walking, running, golfing, and so on. Those are great physical outlets that may rev up your body and focus on movement. The three strategies in this chapter are about slowing down: (1) getting quiet, (2) journaling, and (3) connecting with a colleague. They're simple strategies. But they take just as much discipline to work into your daily routine as the physical workouts. Here's the bottom line: you can't take care of your school if you're not taking care of yourself.

Get Quiet

That's it. Find ten minutes each day to simply sit in silence, or if you're comfortable with the term, meditate. It's a way to get beneath the noise, where things are quiet and clear. Don't race through your work each week; do rest from your work with some quiet time. Shut off your phone. Stay off social media. Take ten minutes to sit in a comfortable position and listen to your breathing. Relax your body. Relax your mind. Recharge. Know that these quiet moments restore your nervous system, help sustain your energy, and facilitate more adaptive and creative thinking (Zorn & Marz, 2017).

These quiet moments have become a small renewal for me each day. My favorite quiet time is first thing in the morning while coffee is brewing. I began setting my alarm ten minutes earlier. Some people prefer to have their quiet time at night to end their day. You know what works for you. Those ten minutes of quiet in the morning have created such a beautiful start to my day that I've continued to extend the time, increasing it a few minutes each morning. More quiet moments have found their way into my life since I began turning off the radio on my way to and from work, walking outside without my earbuds for podcasts, turning off the evening news, and trying an app with beautiful meditative sounds. Be cognizant of the hectic, stress-filled days of your life as a principal. Consider how effective leaders use structured periods of silence as important factors in their success (Zorn & Marz, 2017).

Not only can the quiet time be a catalyst for renewing your energy, but it can also become a time of reflection. If there's something on your mind, you may be amazed at the feeling of release that comes in the quiet moments and the new ideas and solutions that come. Just being disciplined enough to take ten minutes each morning (or anytime) to close off the world, and everyone in it, can bring more rewards than you can imagine.

These ten minutes can create a spaciousness for your spirit to rest and settle. Through moments of going inward into silence, you can grow a bit each day into becoming the kind of leader you want to be. You can quit identifying with all the thoughts running around in your head; you can create a gap in the stream of those thoughts and let a little light flow into your thinking. These quiet moments can become such a powerful antidote to the effects of stress. Your mind can become calm, and your body can become still. That peacefulness can last long after your ten minutes of quiet.

You are bound to get worn down in your leadership and must have a way to shake off the heaviness. You can't fully show up for people until you show up for yourself. If you begin to have trouble sleeping, or sense more fatigue, or find yourself becoming more irritable, these ten minutes of quiet are essential. You give so much of yourself to your school, family, and other activities. Your outer world is filled to the brim with things to do, places to be, people to call, and much more. That's why it's so important to turn inward. The work of stopping, getting quiet, and resting your mind is an inside job. You need the rest and renewal. You need time each day to shape your attitude and your perceptions. You can't always be giving to others. Nourish yourself through daily moments of quiet.

Building nourishing habits is essential for your leadership. This habit of quiet each day, like any worthy habit, can guide your life to a much better destination. And choosing not to build healthy habits, even in small ways, affects your life too. As author James Clear (2018) explains:

> [A choice] that is 1 percent better or 1 percent worse seems insignificant in the moment, but over the span of moments that make up a lifetime these choices determine the difference between who you are and who you could be. Success is the product of daily habits. (pp. 17–18)

Start now to build your healthy habit of getting quiet each day.

One of my favorite articles is titled "Leadership and the New Pope" (Lencioni, 2013), and I've probably read it more than twenty times. Its message continues to resonate with me. It describes what happens immediately after a new pope is elected. The pope, once elected, is escorted into the Room of Tears, just off the Sistine Chapel, where he can be by himself for a while before being introduced to the thousands of exuberant people in St. Peter's Square. The pope spends time there alone in the quiet space to come to grips with the responsibility just placed upon him.

He sits in the silence.

It was reported that Pope Francis sat in the quiet and wept (Lencioni, 2013)—thus, I imagine, the name of the room. He was intentionally stepping aside for a few moments to gather his thoughts, to accept his new position, and to prepare himself for the work ahead. He was looking inward, choosing some moments of silence, and praying about the work and growth he knew he would need.

And that's what we, as school leaders, need to do. Look inward. Get in the silence. Find time to recharge. Become resilient. Reflect. Humbly step forward to do the work. Keep our focus on those we serve.

Journal

So much information has become available about journaling. But one of the most interesting pieces of information is that journaling can lead to a more positive psychological state. Author and writer for *Time* magazine Eric Barker (2014) suggests that people who rate themselves as happy or joyful do not believe there is a happiness *set point*—that is, a point based on your genetics or heredity that determines how happy you can be. Instead, his research shows that people can choose to increase their happiness by developing positive habits (Barker, 2014).

Achor (2011) recommends that people adopt the habit of journaling to keep a more positive state of mind. His advice is to keep it simple by jotting down three things you're grateful for each day. Think of three new things each day, and write them down in your journal. Keep doing this for as long as it takes until it's become a habit. This practice not only focuses your mind on the good in your life but also has a ripple effect and pours out to the people around you.

Journaling with gratitude has been a life changer for me. I use short, bulleted entries that help me look at the abundance all around me. When I began focusing on the good and looking for things I'm grateful for to write in my journal, there just seemed to be more and more of them. What I focused on increased. My focus shifted. I quit looking for things to go wrong or people to say negative things because when you look for the negative, you sure do find it. I don't write every single day, but I've been keeping a gratitude journal for years now, and I consistently write in it four to five times a week. These journals have become some of my most prized possessions.

Another focus for your journaling, other than gratitude, is reflection. I really enjoy responding to writing prompts such as the following to guide me into reflecting about things.

- Where could I have been better this week?
- Think of a person or situation at school that's on your mind. Consider these questions: What can I give here? How can I be of service to this person or situation to move things in a positive direction?

Has keeping a journal changed me as a person? I think so. Has it changed my leadership within my work? I know so. It's been such a benefit to me that as I consult with principals, I present each of them with a journal at our first session together. I explain the benefits of journaling and my personal experiences. We begin by writing down three gratitude items. Then we move into the essential leadership actions and skills, taking lots of notes. But each session after that starts with our opening activity together of pulling out our journals to write about gratitude or reflection. A few principals I've worked with have shared how they've begun to take this habit of journaling to heart. Several of them have begun journaling each day, but most of them have decided to write once a week, on Friday or Saturday, to help bring closure to the week's happenings. Start today. Allow this strategy to bring a short, but powerful, time of renewal and reflection into your leadership.

Connect With a Colleague

This strategy is all about choosing and staying connected with one trusted administrator or colleague, or two if you're lucky. Find a trusted fellow administrator who will stretch your thinking and disagree with you when needed. Meet regularly for support and growth in your leadership. When Learning Forward (2019), a professional learning association, asked principals how they manage stress so they can be resilient and effective, this strategy of connecting with other school leaders was at the top of the list. "No one knows the joys and challenges like others walking in your shoes" (Learning Forward, 2019). So choosing a fellow administrator who understands the job and is capable of helping you turn inward to care for yourself is critical.

Your school leader colleagues are "an invaluable source of support, ideas, resources, inspiration, and feedback" (Learning Forward, 2019). Fellow administrators can share firsthand accounts of things going on in your schools and real situations you can problem solve together. The tough part of this strategy may be finding that person or two. Several colleagues of mine have said that it's not easy to find someone who shares your administrative experiences and, at the same time, guards your conversations with total confidentiality. The principalship can be a lonely job. You need someone with whom you can discuss things openly, someone who sees things from a different perspective, and someone who offers and can benefit from friendship. If you struggle to find someone in your own district, try making a connection in a nearby district or through your state or province's professional organization.

It was important for me to have a fellow principal who understood my frustrations, challenges, and passion for leading a school. Through our conversations, we both got better together. We laughed. We cried. (Well, I did. She's not a crier.) We read. We listened to podcasts. We asked questions. We supported each other in our visions. Being a principal is not about being autonomous or being solitary. It's not about having all the answers; no one does. Being a principal should involve having a trusted colleague so you can share your concerns and fears. You can share your successes and receive genuine feelings of support.

You grow from these conversations together and use them to become a better leader. You learn from your colleague. You grow with your colleague. You have an outlet. This sounding board and this relationship can help you look inward and care for yourself.

In chapter 2 (page 29), we discussed the development of your principal playbook, where you, along with your leadership team, determine the most critical work to accomplish in the upcoming semester at your school. As we discuss looking inward in this chapter, I encourage you to consider the development of your own personal playbook for each semester. You, like any leader, have areas where you can make your leadership even better. Beginning with this focus of turning inward and chapter 9's focus of leaning into the positive (page 143) could be great places to start. You could use items like not thinking the worst before actually finding out the facts, priming your brain before difficult situations, holding on to positive thoughts, growing a more consistent mindset, getting quiet each day, journaling three times a week, or meeting with a trusted colleague monthly. I keep my personal playbook in my personal journal. I add all kinds of notes from my reading time, quiet time revelations, and conversations throughout the semester. It keeps me focused on the right inner work I'm trying to accelerate. Your personal playbook for first semester could look something like figure 10.1.

What	By When	Metric
Begin journaling three times each week. Use positive experiences and things I'm grateful for that week.	December 15	Journal entries
Reflect on the question, Where could I have been more? at the end of each week. Jot down my thoughts for school and home in my journal.	December 15	Journal entries
Find ten minutes each day to sit in the silence and concentrate only on my breathing. Try to clear my thoughts and calm my mind.	December 31	Journal chart of days I accomplished the 10 minutes
Before each monthly central district committee meeting, spend three to four minutes alone, priming my brain before entering the room.	December 10 (last district meeting of the semester)	Journal notes on any success

Figure 10.1: Example personal playbook for the semester.

Give Your Brain a Break

All leaders are at risk of getting burned out from the stressors in these administrative positions. Your students need brain breaks and recess in order to perform at their best. You need brain breaks, too, in order to serve at your best. If you're not already doing them, try these strategies of getting quiet, journaling, and connecting with a colleague. Put some focus on yourself and turn inward to become an even better leader.

To reflect on turning inward and begin work on your next steps, see the reproducible tools on pages 166–168. And turn to page 169 for a tool to help you reflect on and determine next steps for all of part 2.

Personal Playbook Template

Reflect on the three strategies presented in this chapter.

1. Get quiet.

2. Journal.

3. Connect with a colleague.

Use the following template to begin your own personal playbook with these strategies. Feel free to use any of the six tools from chapter 9 (page 143).

What	By When	Metric

Get Quiet and Just Breathe: Two Exercises

When I began taking ten minutes to sit in the silence, I remember that those ten minutes felt like thirty minutes. So many thoughts kept racing through my mind—thoughts of things I needed to do at work and at home. Sometimes I couldn't quiet those thoughts, so I'd get frustrated and quit. To keep my mind from wandering away, I began trying to simply pay attention to my breathing. The following two techniques have helped me immensely. Give them a try.

Exercise 1

Sit quietly and in a comfortable position. Close your eyes. Begin breathing slowly in and out. Take a few breaths. Then, on your inhale, mentally say the word in the left column of the following table. On your exhale, mentally say the word in the right column. Try to breathe naturally, and try to be mindful.

Notice that the first two word sets, in-out and deep-slow, focus on your breathing. The next two word sets, calm-ease and smile-release, focus on your state of being. And the last word set helps you focus on the present moment. When you've finished the five word sets, begin again until your time is up. You may close with a prayer or whatever feels best for you.

Inhale	Exhale
In	Out
Deep	Slow
Calm	Ease
Smile	Release
Present moment	Wonderful moment

Exercise 2

Another breathing technique that keeps my mind from wandering off to my to-do list is this: I simply concentrate on my breathing. This exercise has you mentally count as you breathe. Breathe in for one count; breathe out for one count (see the following table). Breathe in a bit longer while mentally counting one, two; breathe out while mentally counting one, two, and so on. Your breathing should slow down, and you become more at ease. When you get to the last row, you're breathing in very slowly and mentally counting one, two, three, four, five. Then breathe out slowly, while mentally counting one, two, three, four, five. This counting will help keep your thoughts from wandering and bring you back to your breath.

Inhale	Exhale
One	One
One, two	One, two
One, two, three	One, two, three
One, two, three, four	One, two, three, four
One, two, three, four, five	One, two, three, four, five

Source: Adapted from Nhat Hanh, T. (2015) The heart of the Buddha's teaching. New York: Harmony Books.

Journal Ideas: Clear Your Mind of Clutter

Try to prioritize time to write in your journal several times a week. Here are a few writing prompts to get you going. Once you begin journaling for a bit, you'll probably find your own rhythm and style and know exactly what works best for you. It's all about getting quiet and finding time for reflection.

Write down three things you're grateful for today.

1. _____

2. _____

3. _____

Think about a person you'd like to thank for some action or kindness to you or others. Write down a few sentences you could text, email, or say to that person. Then do it!

What is one thing racing around in your mind that's troubling you and you can't seem to stop thinking about? Pause for a few minutes. Think about a few things you could do to feel better about the situation. Jot down a few notes to help ease your mind and enable you to move on to thinking of other positive things.

Part 2 Final Reflection and Next Steps: Essential Leadership Skills—Be Courageous!

As a culminating reflection exercise for part 2, take time to think about all the essential leadership skills and how you can incorporate them into your practice. Then select one or two skills you would like to focus on—you can choose a main skill (shown in bold), some subskills, or both—and use the following template to record instances when you notice your courageous self implementing them. Return to this template on a weekly or biweekly basis to track your progress and adjust your actions as needed.

Essential Leadership Skill 1: Build Relationships

Subskills	When and How I Implemented Them
Build trust.	
Be vulnerable.	
Be cautious of predictive trust.	
Be cautious of the fundamental attribution error.	
Be reliable.	
Have difficult conversations.	
Use the real dialogue model.	
Create your top-ten expectations.	
Ensure your people find meaning in their work.	
Make certain each staff member is known to you, is relevant to the school, and has measurable goals.	

Essential Leadership Skill 2: Reframe Conflict

Subskills	When and How I Implemented Them
Accept that conflict will be part of your leadership.	
Mine for conflict.	
Acknowledge others who address conflict.	
Understand that conflict requires tough decisions.	
Use the four steps of difficult decision making.	

Essential Leadership Skill 3: Hold People Accountable

Subskills	When and How I Implemented Them
Secure commitment from your staff.	
Remember the Golden Circle, and start with *why*.	
Develop parallel accountability (principal to teachers, teachers to teachers, teachers to students).	
Recognize both quantitative and qualitative accountability measures.	

Essential Leadership Skill 4: Lean Into the Positive

Subskills	When and How I Implemented Them
Use tool 1: standing in the gap.	
Use tool 2: choosing a growth mindset.	
Use tool 3: holding the positive.	
Use tool 4: using the expectancy theory.	
Use tool 5: watching your emotions.	
Use tool 6: priming your brain.	

Essential Leadership Skill 6: Turn Inward

Subskills	When and How I Implemented Them
Get quiet (for renewal and reflection).	
Journal (for gratitude and reflection).	
Connect with a colleague.	
Develop your personal playbook.	

Closing

We've looked at five essential leadership actions and five essential leadership skills. Why is it that so many principals don't take advantage of these essential leadership actions and skills? Why do they not understand how much better our schools could be? I'm afraid that many principals do not hold a balanced view of their leadership. Many lean heavily into the leadership actions without giving much thought to the leadership skills, believing the skills are secondary to the actions. Other principals lean heavily into one or two of the skills but don't do the hard work of embedding the essential actions into their school. Principal leadership is not an *either-or* with these actions and skills. It's a *both*! Why do so many principals choose not to maintain a balance in their use of the actions *and* the skills? Let's take a look at four reasons.

1. **Maybe some principals don't incorporate the skills because they believe the leadership skills are not sophisticated enough:** Maybe they believe they're pretty good people, so the leadership skills should just come naturally. Let me be very clear. These essential leadership skills do not come naturally. It takes a deliberate and courageous principal to create a work environment infused with trust, conflict, and accountability. It takes a brave leader who intentionally leans into the positive and looks inward to continually improve. This work may look unsophisticated to some, but it is among the most complex and exhausting.

2. **Maybe some principals believe the results from using these leadership actions and skills are not quantifiable:** It's difficult to show data on how much your staff members trust each other, how skilled they are in handling conflict, and how much you've grown in becoming more positive and looking inward. It's also hard to quantify the actions of clarifying the essential work, creating the right teams to move the work forward, and facilitating worthy meetings. Principals can use student achievement results to quantify these skills and actions, but they can also use teacher interviews as data to show improvement in most of these areas. When these essential leadership skills and actions are truly in place, the school becomes healthy, teachers feel empowered, and students learn at higher levels. People want to work at the school, and people stay there. There are some data.

3. **Maybe some principals think they're just too busy:** I hear this quite often. Principals *are* busy. The all-important position of being a principal is difficult, complex, and multifaceted. But you must choose where and how you manage your time. You can be busy all day long and not accomplish anything of value for your school. Your time must be on the essential work of establishing a vision, clarifying the essential work, creating the right teams to move the work forward, building the proper systems and managing every minute of time, and leading effective meetings. You can never become too busy to lead your school with building relationships, reframing conflict, holding your staff accountable, leaning into the positive, and turning inward. You're never too busy to know how students are learning in your school.

4. **Maybe some principals experience fear:** Yes, fear. As I have worked hard to establish trust with the principals I'm honored to consult with, a few have shared that they just aren't sure they are capable of doing this work. If they do get these essential actions and skills more embedded, they are afraid the actions or skills won't work and they won't get results—understandable fears. I appreciate the vulnerability of these principals in sharing their self-doubts. What's interesting is that these exact principals have demonstrated the most ability in leading their schools through the actions and skills. They are leading their schools to higher academic achievement each year.

Don't allow any of these reasons—the work doesn't seem sophisticated enough, or the results seem too hard to quantify, or you're too busy, or you're too afraid—to stop you from doing this most important work for your staff and students. Be the kind of principal who knows how to balance both the deliberate actions and the courageous skills.

You can do this work. Keep your focus. Keep the negative messages out of your head. You're not a fraud. There's no need to panic anymore like I used to do. You know what you're doing. You've got a plan.

In 1993, I was enrolled in the Experiential Program for Preparing School Principals (EPPSP) at Butler University in Indianapolis, Indiana. This demanding two-year program would prepare our cohort of twenty-one individuals to become school principals. I had successfully completed my first year, but I had come to the decision that I could not complete the program. I had some really good reasons. I had two young children; I was working full-time as a high school guidance counselor; I was in the midst of a devastating divorce; and I didn't have any family living close by to help. I wrote a letter to my professor and asked to see him after class one evening.

As we sat in his office, he opened the letter and began reading. I started spewing my entire life story at him and could barely speak for sobbing. I explained that I simply couldn't remain in the program. Every minute of the first year had been exceptional, but it was too much for me. Besides, I wasn't sure I was cut out to be a principal anyway.

After he handed me a final tissue, we sat in the silence for a couple of minutes. He stared at me while I wiped my face.

"Are you finished talking now?" he asked.

"Yes, I think I've told you everything," I sniffled.

"Well then," he said.

In silence, he stood up from his desk, tore my letter in two right down the middle, and threw both pieces in the trash can with a big slam-dunk motion.

"I don't accept your letter. I don't accept your excuses. I believe in you. You can do this. See you in class on Tuesday night." And with that, he walked out of the office and left me sitting there with a lapful of tissues.

I went back on Tuesday night and completed the final year of the program.

I paraphrase some of his words to you here: I don't accept your reasons or excuses. I believe in you. You can do this. You can be deliberate and courageous. And our schools, more than ever in my lifetime, need you to do this. Your time is now. Do it for your school. Your staff. Your students. Your leadership.

References and Resources

Achor, S. (2011). *The happiness advantage: The seven principles that fuel success and performance at work.* London: Virgin.

Ainsworth, L. (2010). *Rigorous curriculum design: How to create curricular units of study that align standards, instruction, and assessment.* Englewood, CA: Lead + Learn Press.

Ainsworth, L. (2014). *Common formative assessments 2.0: How teacher teams intentionally align standards, instruction, and assessment* (2nd ed.). Thousand Oaks, CA: Corwin Press.

Bailey, C., & Madden, A. (2016). What makes work meaningful—or meaningless. *MIT Sloan Management Review, 57*(4), 53–61.

Balch, B., & Brower, R. (2005). *Transformational leadership and decision making in schools.* Thousand Oaks, CA: Corwin Press.

Barker, E. (2014, October 15). *Success.* Accessed at https://goodthinkinc.com/project/success-you-have-the-power-to-lead-with-positivity on June 21, 2021.

Brown, B. (2007). *I thought it was just me: Women reclaiming power and courage in a culture of shame.* New York: Gotham.

Brown, B. (2017). *Braving the wilderness: The quest for true belonging and the courage to stand alone.* New York: Random House.

Brown, B. (2018). *Dare to lead: Brave work. Tough conversations. Whole hearts.* New York: Random House.

Buckingham, M. (2005). *The one thing you need to know: About great managing, great leading, and sustained individual success.* New York: Free Press.

Clear, J. (n.d.a). *The mistake smart people make: Being in motion vs. taking action* [Blog post]. Accessed at https://jamesclear.com/taking-action on February 15, 2021.

Clear, J. (n.d.b). *Rome wasn't built in a day, but they were laying bricks every hour* [Blog post]. Accessed at https://jamesclear.com/lay-a-brick on February 15, 2021.

Clear, J. (2018). *Atomic habits: Tiny changes, remarkable results—An easy and proven way to build good habits and break bad ones.* New York: Avery.

Collins, J. (2001). *Good to great: Why some companies make the leap—and others don't.* New York: HarperBusiness.

Courage. (n.d.). In *The American heritage dictionary of the English language.* Accessed at https://ahdictionary.com/word/search.html?q=courage#:~:text=n.,confidence%2C%20and%20resolution%3B%20bravery on February 15, 2021.

Crum, A. J., & Langer, E. J. (2007). Mind-set matters: Exercise and the placebo effect. *Psychological Science, 18*(2), 165–171.

Diaz, C. (2017, December 31). *Why Maya Angelou's lesson on courage is more important than ever* [Blog post]. Accessed at https://blog.mindvalley.com/importance-of-courage on June 17, 2021.

Dougherty, B. J., Bush, S. B., & Karp, K. S. (2020). *The math pact, high school: Achieving instructional coherence within and across grades.* Thousand Oaks, CA: Corwin Press.

Doyle, G. (2020). *Untamed.* New York: Dial Press.

DuFour, R., & DuFour, R. (2012, October 15). *Part 1: Beware of seductive shortcuts on the PLC journey* [Webinar]. Accessed at www.solutiontree.com/plc-at-work-web-series-ewp023.html on September 2, 2020.

DuFour, R., DuFour, R., Eaker R., Many, T. W., & Mattos, M. (2016). *Learning by doing: A handbook for Professional Learning Communities at Work* (3rd ed.). Bloomington, IN: Solution Tree Press.

DuFour, R., & Eaker, R. (1998) *Professional Learning Communities at Work: Best practices for enhancing student achievement.* Bloomington, IN: Solution Tree Press.

DuFour, R., & Marzano, R. (2011). *Leaders of learning: How district, school, and classroom leaders improve student achievement.* Bloomington, IN: Solution Tree Press.

Dweck, C. (2017). *Mindset: Changing the way you think to fulfill your potential* (Updated ed.). London: Robinson.

Eaker, R., & Reeves, D. (2020, Summer). Building Professional Learning Communities at Work through 100-day cycles. *AllThingsPLC Magazine,* 10–16.

Everett, A. (2018, February 13). *Coach wants to see you . . . bring your playbook* [Blog post]. Accessed at www.linkedin.com/pulse/coach-wants-see-you-bring-your-playbook-al-everett on February 15, 2021.

Explorance. (2020, May 26). *Discovering the 4 panes of the Johari Window for 360 degree feedback* [Blog post]. Accessed at https://explorance.com/blog/discovering-blind-spots-in-360-degree-feedback-with-the-johari-window on June 19, 2021.

Feirsen, R., & Weitzman, S. (2021). Constructive conflict. *Educational Leadership, 78*(7), 26–31.

Gawande, A. (2009). *The checklist manifesto: How to get things right.* New York: Metropolitan Books.

Gielan, M. (2015). *Broadcasting happiness: The science of igniting and sustaining positive change.* Dallas, TX: BenBella Books.

Gielan, M. (2016). *Broadcasting happiness* [Ebook]. Accessed at http://goodthinkinc.com/wp-content/uploads/2016/01/Broadcasting-Happiness-eBook1.pdf on November 5, 2020.

Goleman, D. (2006a). *Emotional intelligence* (10th anniversary hardcover ed.). New York: Bantam Books.

Goleman, D. (2006b). *Social intelligence: The new science of human relationships.* New York: Bantam Books.

Goleman, D. (2019). *The emotionally intelligent leader.* Boston: Harvard Business Review Press.

Graham, J. (n.d.). *#5—The importance of vision* [Blog post]. Accessed at www.johngraham.org/coach/5-the-importance-of-vision on August 31, 2018.

Grissom, J., Egalite, A., & Lindsay, C. (2021). *How principals affect students and schools: A systematic synthesis of two decades of research.* New York: The Wallace Foundation. Accessed at www.wallacefoundation.org/principalsythesis on July 19, 2021.

Gruenert, S. (2019, July 9). *Culture matters* [Keynote address]. Indiana Principal Leadership Institute, Terre Haute, IN.

Gruenert, S., & Whitaker, T. (2015). *School culture rewired: How to define, assess, and transform it.* Alexandria, VA: Association for Supervision and Curriculum Development.

Hanig, R., & Senge, P. (2015, September 29). *Leadership frameworks* [Conference presentation]. Society for Organizational Learning workshop, Ashland, MA.

Hanson, R. (2013). *Hardwiring happiness: The new brain science of contentment, calm, and confidence.* New York: Harmony Books.

Hanson, R. (2014) *Taking in the good vs. the negativity bias.* Accessed at www.sfsu.edu/~holistic/documents/Spring_2014/GoodvsNeg_Bias.pdf on June 19, 2021.

Hattie, J. (2018, May 1). *Hattie: Collective efficacy on Vimeo—Challenging learning* [Video file]. Accessed at https://vimeo.com/267382804 on June 29, 2021.

Hoff, N. (2020, August 26). *Preparing for uncertainty.* Accessed at https://smartbrief.com/original/2020/08/preparing-uncertainty?utm_source=brief on May 28, 2021.

Holden, K. (2018). *What do we know about the importance of principals for student achievement?* (CALDER Policy Brief No. 10-0918-1). Washington, DC: National Center for Analysis of Longitudinal Data in Education Research. Accessed at http://caldercouncil.org/what-do-we-know-about-the-importance-of-principals-for-student-achievement/#.X2dWUtNKg6U on September 20, 2020.

Inspiritory. (2017, September 21). *Empathy—Best speech of all time by Simon Sinek* [Video file]. Accessed at www.youtube.com /watch?v=IJyNoJCAuzA&t=42s&mc_cid=42e5ea3b6d&mc_eid=91251ddffe on February 16, 2021.

Jones, C., & Doren, K. (2001). *That's outside my boat: Letting go of what you can't control.* Kansas City, MO: Andrews McMeel.

Knight, J. (2017, July 31). *Trust—an essential part of coaching* [Video file]. Accessed at https://instructionalcoaching.com/trust -essential-part-coaching on July 31, 2017.

Landry, L. (2019, April 3). *Why emotional intelligence is important in leadership* [Blog post]. Accessed at https://online.hbs.edu /blog/post/emotional-intelligence-in-leadership on June 16, 2021.

Lead. (n.d.). In *The American heritage dictionary of the English language.* Accessed at https://ahdictionary.com/word/search .html?q=lead on February 15, 2021.

Learning Forward. (2019). How school leaders manage stress and stay focused. *The Learning Professional, 40*(5). Accessed at https://learningforward.org/journal/resilient-leadership/how-school-leaders-manage-stress-and-stay-focused on November 17, 2020.

Lencioni, P. (2002). *The five dysfunctions of a team: A leadership fable.* San Francisco: Jossey-Bass.

Lencioni, P. (2007). *The three signs of a miserable job: A fable for managers (and their employees).* San Francisco: Jossey-Bass.

Lencioni, P. (2012). *The advantage: Why organizational health trumps everything else in business.* San Francisco: Jossey-Bass.

Lencioni, P. (2013, March). *Leadership and the new pope* [Blog post]. Accessed at www.tablegroup.com/hub/post/leadership -and-the-new-pope on June 12, 2018.

Lencioni, P. (2017, May 16). *Fundamental attribution error* [Video file]. Accessed at www.youtube.com/watch?v=82-qnZMcfm0 on February 15, 2021.

Levine, B. N. (2016, June 30). *Push vs. pull: Why your communication style matters* [Blog post]. Accessed at www.amanet.org /articles/push-pull-communication-style-matters on February 15, 2021.

Marshall, K. (2008). The big rocks: Priority management for principals. *Principal Leadership, 8*(7), 16–22. Accessed at https://marshallmemo.com/articles/Time%20Management%20PL%20Mar%2008.pdf on February 15, 2021.

Marshall, K. (2019, February 20). *Rethinking the way we coach, evaluate, and appreciate teachers* [Blog post]. Accessed at https://fordhaminstitute.org/national/commentary/rethinking-way-we-coach-evaluate-and-appreciate-teachers on November 12, 2020.

Marshall, K., & Marshall, D. (2017). Mini-observations: A keystone habit. *School Administrator, 74*(11), 26–29.

Marzano, R. J., Warrick, P., & Simms, J. A. (2014). *A handbook for High Reliability Schools: The next step in school reform.* Bloomington, IN: Marzano Resources.

Master, J. C., Barden, R. C., & Ford, M. C. (1979). Affective states, expressive behavior, and learning in children. *Journal of Personality and Social Psychology, 37*, 380–390.

Maxwell, J. (2010). *Everyone communicates, few connect: What the most effective people do differently.* Nashville, TN: Nelson.

Molinaro, V. (2018). *The leadership contract: The fine print to becoming an accountable leader* (3rd ed.). Hoboken, NJ: Wiley.

Muhammad, A. (2018). *Transforming school culture: How to overcome staff division* (2nd ed.). Bloomington, IN: Solution Tree Press.

Nhat Hanh, T. (2015) *The heart of the Buddha's teaching.* New York: Harmony Books.

Nordic Business Forum. (2018, February 4). *Patrick Lencioni: "Build vulnerability-based trust on your teams" (part 2)* [Video file]. Accessed at www.youtube.com/watch?v=ACCn1sNYpVc on February 15, 2021.

Pink, D. (2018). *When: The scientific secrets of perfect timing.* New York: Riverhead Books.

Pink, D. (2019, November 25). *Optimizing performance* [Keynote address]. Indiana Association of School Principals fall conference, Indianapolis, IN.

Richardson, J. (2016). *The next step forward in guided reading: An assess-decide-guide framework for supporting every reader, grades K–8.* New York: Scholastic.

Rohr, R. (Host). (2017, December 17). The Velcro/Teflon explanation [Audio podcast episode]. *Homilies.* Accessed at https://cac.org/podcasts/velcro-teflon-explanation on February 16, 2021.

Romero, C. (2015, July). *What we know about growth mindset from scientific research.* Accessed at http://studentexperiencenetwork.org/wp-content/uploads/2015/09/What-We-Know-About-Growth-Mindset.pdf on June 20, 2021.

Rutherford Learning Group. (n.d.). *Leadership notes: Peter Drucker on organized abandonment.* Accessed at https://rutherfordlg.com/rlg_new/wp-content/uploads/2016/08/Leadership-Notes-Peter-Drucker-on-Organized-Abandonment120517-1.pdf on June 20, 2021.

Schmitz, T. W., De Rosa, E., & Anderson, A. K. (2009). Opposing influences of affective state valence on visual cortical encoding. *Journal of Neuroscience, 29,* 7199–7207.

Schmoker, M. (2004). Learning communities at the crossroads: Toward the best schools we've ever had. *Phi Delta Kappan, 86*(1), 84–89.

Schmoker, M. (2011). *Focus: Elevating the essentials to radically improve student learning.* Alexandria, VA: Association for Supervision and Curriculum Development.

Shepard, D. (Host). (2020, August 13). Atul Gawande (No. 234) [Audio podcast episode]. *Armchair Expert.* Accessed at https://armchairexpertpod.com/pods/atul-gawande on February 15, 2021.

Shutack, C. (2017, August 13). *103 things white people can do for racial justice.* Accessed at https://medium.com/equality-includes-you/what-white-people-can-do-for-racial-justice-f2d18b0e0234 on June 16, 2021.

Sinek, S. (2009). *Start with why: How great leaders inspire everyone to take action.* New York: Portfolio.

Sinek, S. (2017). *Find your why: A practical guide for discovering purpose for you or your team.* New York: Portfolio.

Super Soul Sunday. (2011, November 30). *Take responsibility for your energy* [Video file]. Accessed at www.youtube.com/watch?v=T81a6zcQpHc on June 10, 2020.

Talks at Google. (2015, July 16). *The growth mindset: Carol Dweck* [Video file]. Accessed at www.youtube.com/watch?v=6WbqxKUS9eQ on August 1, 2019.

Van Soelen, T. M. (2021). *Meeting goals: Protocols for leading effective, purpose driven discussions in schools.* Bloomington, IN: Solution Tree Press.

Vroom, V. H. (1964). *Work and motivation.* New York: Wiley.

Warrick, P. (2020, September 23). *Cultivating effective teaching in every classroom* [Virtual keynote address]. Indiana Principal Leadership Institute.

Watkins, A. (2016). *Role of the principal in beginning teacher induction* [Practice brief]. Santa Cruz, CA: New Teacher Center. Accessed at https://newteachercenter.org/wp-content/uploads/Role-of-Principal-in-Teacher-Induction.pdf on February 1, 2021.

Whitaker, T. (2020). *What great principals do differently: Twenty things that matter most* (3rd ed.). New York: Routledge.

Whitaker, T., Whitaker, M., & Whitaker, K. (2016). *Your first year: How to survive and thrive as a new teacher.* New York: Routledge.

Wiliam, D. (2011). *Embedded formative assessment.* Bloomington, IN: Solution Tree Press.

Williams, K. C., & Hierck, T. (2015). *Starting a movement: Building culture from the inside out in professional learning communities.* Bloomington, IN: Solution Tree Press.

World of Business Ideas. (2012, June 18). *My definition of leadership: Peter Senge* [Video file]. Accessed at https://conversational-leadership.net/video/video-peter-senge-leadership on August 25, 2020.

Wright, K. (2018, February 22). *What your ch'i says about you.* Accessed at https://leadingwright.com/2018/02/22/leadership-message-what-your-chi-says-about-you on December 12, 2020.

Zorn, J. T., & Marz, L. (2017, March 17). The busier you are, the more you need quiet time. *Harvard Business Review.* Accessed at https://hbr.org/2017/03/the-busier-you-are-the-more-you-need-quiet-time on February 15, 2021.

Index

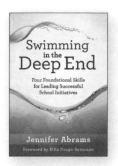

Swimming in the Deep End
Jennifer Abrams

Acquire the knowledge and resources necessary to lead successful change initiatives in schools. In *Swimming in the Deep End*, author Jennifer Abrams dives deep into the four foundational skills required of effective leadership and provides ample guidance for cultivating each.

BKF830

Connecting Through Leadership
Jasmine K. Kullar

The success of a school greatly depends on the ability of its leaders to communicate effectively. Rely on *Connecting Through Leadership* to help you strengthen your communication skills to inspire, motivate, and connect with every member of your school community.

BKF927

Leading the Launch
Kim Wallace

How do schools and districts make true progress? One step at a time. *Leading the Launch* offers a ten-stage initiative implementation process proven to help you lead the charge for change with ingenuity, flexibility, responsiveness, and passion.

BKG030

Doing What Works
Chris Weber

While new ideas and innovative programs and pedagogies are exciting, the simplest methods are often the most effective. In *Doing What Works*, author Chris Weber outlines ten practical, common-sense practices proven to transform student learning and propel school success.

BKF916

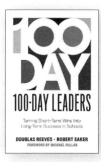

100-Day Leaders
Douglas Reeves and Robert Eaker

Within 100 days, schools can dramatically increase student achievement, transform faculty morale, reduce discipline issues, and much more. Using *100-Day Leaders* as a guide, you will learn how to achieve a series of short-term wins that combine to form long-term success.

BKF919

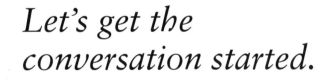